A CONFLUENCE
OF WITCHES

A CONFLUENCE OF WITCHES

*Celebrating Our Lunar Roots,
Decolonizing the Craft, and Reenchanting Our World*

A MODERN WITCHES ANTHOLOGY

compiled & edited by

CASEY ZABALA

WEISER
BOOKS

This edition first published in 2024 by Weiser Books, an imprint of
Red Wheel/Weiser, LLC
With offices at:
65 Parker Street, Suite 7
Newburyport, MA 01950
www.redwheelweiser.com

ISBN: 978-1-57863-845-1
Library of Congress Cataloging-in-Publication Data available upon request.

Cover design by Sky Peck Design
Interior images by Casey Zabala
Typeset in Celeste

Printed in the United States of America
IBI
10 9 8 7 6 5 4 3 2 1

CONTENTS

Acknowledgments   **ix**

Introduction by Casey Zabala   **1**

Chapter 1
MODERN WITCHES WORSHIP THE MOON   **7**
Through Time, Space & Craft

All Moons Are for All Lifetimes
by Maria Minnis   **10**

Moondance: Lunation Magick in Eight Part Harmony: ArtSpells and Rituals
with Apothecary Provisions for a Full Lunation
by Angela Mary Magick   **19**

Chapter 2:
TRADITIONAL MAGICK AND MODERN TECHNOLOGIES   **33**
Weaving Ancestral Medicine into Digital Webs

Makuyeika: somos de aquí y somos de allá Kawi
by Edgar Fabián Frías   **36**

Roma Futurism: Resilience, Witchcraft, and Technology
by Jezmina Von Thiele   **45**

Reclaiming Resourcing: Money Magic in This Time of Capitalism
by Jessie Susannah Karnatz   **52**

Chapter 3:
DECOLONIZING WITCHCRAFT   59
Reclaiming the Power of Lineage, Mythology, and Sovereignty

Tracing the Thread of Belonging Spell + Ritual
by Kiki Robinson   **62**

There Is Sustenance in the Roots
by Star Feliz   **70**

Preserving the Witch
by Kimberly Rodriguez   **77**

Chapter 4:
WE GATHER IN SPIRIT WORLDS   83
Betwixt and Between Allies, Guides, and Supernatural Wisdom

Creating a Spirit Guide Language:
Strengthening Your Connection to the Unseen Realm
by Aja Daashuur   **86**

There's Something about Mary
by Aurora Luna   **92**

Loving What Is: Quantum Witchcraft
by Sanyu Estelle   **96**

Chapter 5:
WITCHCRAFT, BODY, EARTH   103
Look to the Rhizomes and Mycelium: Situating Your Magic
in Your Relationship with Earth

Flower Animism: A Floral Spell by Liz Migliorelli   **106**

Telling the Bees: Communicating and Relating to the More-Than-Human World
by Ariella Daly   **113**

Taken by Faeries
by Amanda Yates Garcia   **120**

Chapter 6:
HEALING PATHWAYS   **135**
Spells & Meditations on Healing Work

Sacred Rose Healing
by Alejandra Luisa León   **138**

*You're Reading Everyone around You, All the Time: Learning Energetic
Boundaries with the Self and Others, for Readers, Healers, and Witches*
by Rachel Howe   **141**

*Planetary Hours & the Doomsday Clock: On Being Sick & Carrying an Earth-
Based Tradition in a Time of Ecological Calamity*
by olivia pepper   **149**

El Regreso (The Return)
by Madre Jaguar   **164**

Chapter 7
COVEN-WORK   **169**
How to Organize, Gather, and Evolve Together

Herbalism as Mutual Aid
by Damiana   **172**

We Measure the Sea: A Declaration of Art as Magic as Connection
by Eliza Swann   **176**

Witching, Weaving, Casting Spells toward Liberation
A conversation with adrienne maree brown and Dori Midnight   **185**

Contributor Bios   **200**

Acknowledgments

The Modern Witches community is nothing without the witches, edge-walkers, medicine people, intuitives, artists, and activists that attend our events, lead our workshops, organize our events, and share their ideas and spirit with us. A heartfelt thanks to you all, for participating in our community both online and in person. A special deep bow of gratitude to all those who have spent hours creating content with me, selling tickets to our events, managing merchandise tables, pouring tea, building altars, and sweeping auditorium floors. Without all of your enthusiasm for witchcraft, this project would only be a wild seed. Your faith in your own spiritual path empowers this work, inspires me on my own journey, and is the fertile soil required for the deep supportive roots of this community to form. The work we do as an organization is possible because of the collective desire to express and explore our magic together. I am deeply grateful for the opportunity to cast circles with you all and am humbled by the potential of our collaborative spells.

Revolutionary Letter #46

And as you learn the magic, learn to believe it

Don't be surprised when it works, you undercut
your power.

—Diane di Prima

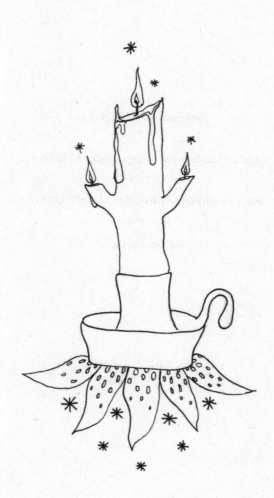

INTRODUCTION

BY CASEY ZABALA

Contrary to popular opinion, witchcraft is not a trend. A trend implies something that is temporarily and cyclically fashionable, while witchcraft is as ancient as the Moon. True, the Moon cycles through its own phases of power and light, and one could argue that witchcraft does just the same, occulting precious aspects of its powerful secrets to protect its adherents, while empowering and emboldening witches to embrace their magical identities when the culture can sustain it. This mutability in itself is core to the lasting power of witchcraft. Witchcraft has been here since the beginning, continuing to shapeshift and create new constellations of meaning as it evolves alongside our modern preoccupations.

The aim of the present anthology is to reconnect a generation of powerful witches to a multitude of pathways of practice, philosophy, and spiritual experience. As I write this, in the depth of Winter in the year 2023, we find ourselves collectively at a Full Moon moment in Witchcraft's cyclical history. More individuals are finding their way back to magical thinking, animism, eco-spirituality, and communing with unseen worlds. More individuals are finding themselves drawn to the idea that we are innately powerful beings, capable of changing our consciousness at will, capable of healing our psyches, and in turn healing our relationship with Earth. More of us are realizing the alchemical properties of believing in magic, believing in something other than the mechanistic paradigm we have all been conditioned by.

Modern Witchcraft is not a disavowal of our Pagan, animist, lunar roots. Rather, Modern Witchcraft is an evolution of our responsibilities as practicing witches. These responsibilities have historically been to praise the divinity of the Earth and cosmos, to provide healing remedy and support to the community, and to offer a spiritual framework for the oppressed. To be a modern witch we must straddle both our ancient origins and our futurist dreams.

While Modern Witchcraft has adopted platforms like TikTok and Instagram for connecting with fellow witches and generating community, we are still aware of the potent threads of energy woven through our workings in the digital realm. Just as it is important to understand the quality of ingredients going into a spell sachet, we also must understand the powers that are behind the social media giants whose algorithms are curating our digital connections. As Modern Witches, we must practice a new wave of technological discernment as we cast spells for a liberated future and take advantage of the accessibility and expansion that new technologies can provide to us. 20th century witchcraft is simultaneously constructed by ancient symbols and encoded messages, psychic hygiene, and digital boundary work.

Genuine witchcraft is an anticapitalist project, aimed at reconnecting or reforging our innate bonds with nature. Nature is not separate from our bodies. Nature is not an external resource to be exploited. In Modern Witchcraft the Moon is our ally, a part of how we connect with ourselves and with the organic cycle of growth and decay. The Moon is known to affect the tides of the great waters that blanket our planet, as well as the tidal flow of blood and water in our bodies. The Moon is a living, changing, spiritual entity that has come to symbolize the divine feminine within each of us, our receptive powers of intuition, and our magical intuitive need for both rest and renewal. The Moon is the witches' most basic ally. The Moon is no more our enemy than we ourselves can become under the calculated project of the patriarchy. The true enemy of Modern Witchcraft are the dominant forces at work, tricking us into believing that the Moon is nothing more than an inanimate piece of space rock reflecting the Sun's light. Our collective adversary are those who wish to indoctrinate us into believing that Earth is not sentient, that we are not innately powerful, capable of generating real change in our own lives and in the lives of others.

It was the Moon in its fullness that initiated my own path into witchcraft. One summer night when I was young, I was woken up by a stream of silvery light flooding into my room. I sat in the window, transfixed by the glowing Moon, who I heard calling out to me by name, calling me home through its luminescence. I was only seven years old at the time, but this moment of direct communion with the Moon forged a sincere and experienced awareness that all aspects of creation are conscious and full of mystery. That initiation by moonlight is an example of one of the many ways witches find themselves on the path of magic, enchantment, and healing. This anthology explores the many ways witchcraft can embolden us to embrace the mysteries of the cosmos, and find ways to co-create changes in our psyches and our societies, no matter how one has stumbled onto the path. . .

With an increase in collective curiosity and sincere devotion to our spiritual practices, comes push-back from the dominant capitalist forces working their own manipulative magic; corporations co-opt spiritual language to leverage capital gains with the intention to keep us securely under their thumbs. Witch-boxes and occult cosmetics. Crystals and white sage sold at Walmart. Abundance gurus and pre-packaged rituals. TikTok witches who brashly cast spells that work against their best efforts to connect with powerful spiritual entities. To survey the landscape of modern witchcraft is to tip-toe through landmines of cultural appropriation and spiritual consumerism, empty promises of healing, freedom, and inner peace. Yet, underneath the dominant culture's smoke and mirrors exists the true spirit of witchcraft, always shapeshifting in conversation with the dominant culture that attempts to corrupt, bind, and demonize it, yet never able to isolate us, nor extinguish the sacred flame. This radical unyielding spirit is what this present anthology aims to illuminate, protect, and empower. This is the radical spirit of Modern Witchcraft.

Witches, or witch-curious allies, are ready to probe deeper into the mystery that is modern witchcraft—to develop our awareness of the diversity of magical paths that can coexist within the ecology of modern spiritual practices. Through our differences we see the gorgeous prism our collective could create if we were to collaborate with reverence and respect. As more of us are discovering who we are as magical beings, as witches, *brujas,* seers, elders, *curanderas,* and more, the more we are challenged to confront the dominant forces that have historically worked to suppress our magic.

If you are reading this anthology, you have in some small yet significant way been called to the path of witchcraft. Once this path looked a very specific way; patchouli scented, wrapped in velvet, and deeply biased by a Eurocentric lens. However, today witchcraft offers us a multitude of archetypes, mythologies, lineages, and practices that speak deeply to our authentic relationship with our magic. The term "witch," while European in origin, has come to encompass a much wider definition of magic and spirituality that includes activists, artists, anarchists, medicine people, queer folks, astrologers, and more. This anthology aims to further illuminate those gorgeously diverse, radically political, and spiritually accepting paths.

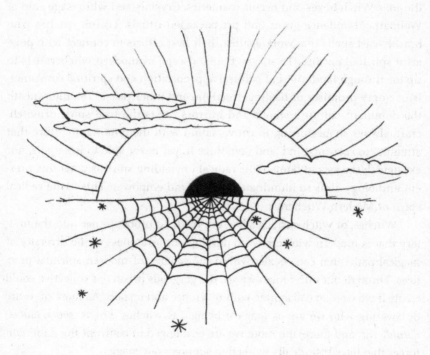

Contributions to this anthology have been made by the following writers: adrienne maree brown, Aja Daashuur, Alejandra Luisa León, Amanda Yates Garcia, Angela Mary Magick, Ariella Daly, Aurora Luna, aka Baby Reckless, Damiana Calvario, Dori Midnight, Edgar Fabián Frías, Eliza Swann, Jessie Susannah Karnatz, Jezmina Von Thiele, Kiki Robinson, Kimberly Rodriguez, Liz Migliorelli, Madre Jaguar, Maria Minnis, Olivia Ephraim Pepper, Rachel Howe, Sanyu Estelle, Star Feliz. The community present in this anthology has been cultivated over the years through live gatherings known as Modern Witches Confluences. Beginning in 2018, we have been bringing together magical minds who work within their own cultural framework of witchcraft, healing, and spirituality. This network of witches has always been an open circle, welcome to anyone who is willing to show up with authenticity, kindness, and inclusivity. Along the way we have challenged ourselves to maintain that radical framework, always working to evolve as an organization alongside the needs of our community.

We welcome you to our sacred circle.

CHAPTER 1

MODERN WITCHES WORSHIP THE MOON

Through Time, Space & Craft

"There is reason, after all, that some people wish to colonize the moon, and others dance before it as an ancient friend."—James Baldwin

WITCHCRAFT IS A LUNAR PRACTICE. Like the Moon, witchcraft flourishes in the darkness. It is ever evolving in its shape and quality of light; it is ancient, primal, ever present. Like the Moon, witchcraft is an essential and mysterious part of our human existence. One could say that the Moon is the first cosmic teacher of all witches. Throughout time witchcraft has taken on many shapes, a constellation of beliefs, myths, and practices. Though these spiritual practices have been ever present throughout history, our perspectives and relationship to witchcraft, just as our relationship to our silver satellite, have shape shifted over time.

My first magical encounter with the Moon was when I was seven years old. Being driven home from a social gathering late one July night, I trained my eyes on the shimmering silver orb, tracing the lace of blacked out pine trees whirling past. Once home and in bed, I couldn't sleep. The light of the Full Moon had flooded my bedroom, filling my body with a new type of wonder. I stayed up most of the night, staring out of my bedroom window, feeling the magnetic purr of the Moon, calling out my name. This was the night I first knew I was a witch.

It wouldn't be until many winding years later that I would formally discover the practice of "drawing down the Moon," a meditation technique in which we call forth the Moon's insights and wisdom, inviting in this lunar intelligence and effectively embodying lunar power. When drawing down the Moon, we become aware of how we hold lunar light within us. The Moon can charge our bodies, our spirits, and our psyches in ways that empower the intuitive, silvery, psychic currents within us.

As witches, the Moon is our collaborator, our teacher, our source of power. The ways in which we engage with and create relationships with the Moon affirm how we are in relationship with our own bodies, each other's bodies, and our essential grasp of natural cycles—death, birth, and renewal. As the Moon changes phase and level of illumination, we too can assess the texture and stories of our own natural cycles of growth and release, emptiness and fullness. When we draw down the Moon and hold her in our bodies, we affirm a basic understanding that all humans are influenced by the Moon. Just like the tides are pulled and pushed by the Moon, so is the water and blood within our bodies.

Enacting a lunar practice is basic and it is revolutionary. Moving through the world with an awareness of lunar phases is a simple act that can change the fabric of your life—both your waking life and your inner worlds. Not only is working with the Moon a personal spiritual practice—it is also a political act.

In astrology, the Moon represents our emotions, our bodies, and people—the collective experience of all of us—the people. The Moon is not only encouraging quiet contemplation and introspection, no, it is encouraging us to recognize how we're all intimately connected on Earth, under our one precious Moon. The Moon pulls on the waters of my body just as it creates the tides, just as it pulls on the blood of your cycle. The Moon inspires intuitive action. With its soft silvery brilliance we are all called on by the Moon—just as we all have the capacity to practice witchcraft. We are all lunar beings with lunar needs, just like we all have the capacity for intuitive knowing. What would happen if we collectively attuned to those intuitive/lunar needs? May the following offerings support you in deepening your lunar practice, through ritual and mythological frameworks.

—Casey

All Moons Are for All Lifetimes

BY MARIA MINNIS

The witch is a multiplicitous figure, a holographic cosmic spiral who casts spells attuned to their complex, ever-changing surroundings. No one controls everything, but everyone can control their responses. The moon revolves around us without any human influence, yet humanity has long been shaped by the moon's many faces. In sympathetic, like-attracts-like magic, witches time shift their ritual and focus based on their surroundings: seasons, dwellings, people, celestial movement—this includes lunar cycles.

We are solar powered and lunar guided. As the sun overtly electrifies our outer bodies and actions, the moon subtly influences our inner selves and how we navigate our lives through intuition, emotion, and spirituality. The sun, our outer reality, illuminates the moon; thus it illuminates our personal relationship to the greater world. Both celestial bodies alter the ocean's tides, but the moon's influence is much stronger as it is about only 238,900 miles away from Earth. The moon doesn't just affect the oceans, but all of the water on Earth—including the water in our bodies. The sun fuels our physical activity, seasons, and sustenance. The moon sways our inner bodies, intimacies that are infinitely connected to all of the water, and thus all of the humans, on this planet. The marriage between the two spheres is inextricable: We are always solar and lunar beings. Ever since our ancestors first gazed at the sky, the lunar cycles have guided the ways we intimately relate to our planet. Shoot for the moon. Moonshine. The man in the moon. Over the moon. Moonlighting. Moon-drops. Lunacy. Honeymoon. Once in a blue moon. Moon child. For generations, people have integrated the moon into everyday language, and thus our everyday lives.

Before Life

Globally, many cultures have linked the moon with varying perspectives of womanhood. As the lunar and menstrual cycles are often around twenty-eight days long, people have long connected our lunar satellite with fertility. Some believe that before the advent of manmade light and chemical contraception, women across the world menstruated around similar times. A study by medical doctor Edson Andrews demonstrated that most bleeding emergencies occurred between the waxing and waning moons, with a notable apex at the full moon. Women living closely together can experience a rhythmic harmony when their menstrual cycles sync within days of each other. If the moon can affect bleeding, we might consider whether the moon speaks to the waxing and waning of our blood-dependent bodies.

Naturopath, herbalist, and author of *Natural Fertility*, Francesca Naish suggests some ways that the moon might affect reproductive faculties:

- Gravitational force. By gravity, an ovum is suspended in fluid. Depending on timing and positioning, the moon's effect on the Earth's gravity encourages ovulation and pushes to release the egg.

- Light availability. The amount of light changes as the moon waxes and wanes. The moon may increase the levels of follicle stimulating hormone, which is critical for ovulation.

- Ionization. While negative ions propagate during the waning moon, the full moon sees an increase in positive ions. This flow especially influences the adrenal glands, which balance ovarian hormones.

- Electromagnetism. The electrical potential of organic beings increases and decreases throughout the lunar cycle, affecting the nervous system.

Feminine lunar folklore extends beyond menstruation. Some ancient societies believed that more births occurred under the full moon, giving the satellite the nickname "the great midwife." The mother archetype nurtures their young, but also all of their other creations. With wisdom, presence, and attentive care, they pay attention to their energetic waxing and waning, intuitively knowing when to intervene or let their child take their course. They are fluid like the moon, eschewing rigidity in favor of cyclical flow. They don't need tight, hierarchical control over their projects because they know the tides will forever rise and fall. Akin to the mother-child relationship, the moon's influence is ever-present, but it's up to us to choose where and how we channel our water. The Moon as Mother is the Moon as care. The moon symbolizes our shared responsibility to use our inherent, flowing creativity to cultivate a world of collective care.

> *. . . I standing on your crescent, madonna, moon,*
> *Old woman that never dies, being perpetually*
> *Renewed, made nothing again, made small again,*
> *Waxing again, going through it all over again,*
> *I would lift up my song, bark, howl, bay to you;*
> *I would say to you, remember me, beloved 3-headed nurse,*
> *I have swallowed your milk, you wiped me and wrapped me;*
> *Beautiful motherly monster, watch over me still.*
>
> —Constance Urdang

Throughout Life

Ever since people have used it to guide plant cultivation, seasonal rituals, having sex, and dreaming of worlds beyond earth, the moon is interwoven throughout many stories of how ancient and modern people navigate life. Cosmology is as old as humankind. Physical cosmology is the study and evolution of the universe, while religious cosmology explains the cosmos based on traditional mythologies. As soon as people developed language, they attempted to articulate the world around them. Early humans anthropomorphized the universe, depicting a living and animate reality. They used rituals, prayers, and sacrifices to gain control of the planetary mysteries. People projected their human emotions and motives as the forces that moved the universe. Between 5,000 and 20,000 years ago, humans developed culture, offering a permanence in daily life that led to cosmic mythologies, many of which explained the origins of celestial bodies. Whether you believe these myths are realistic or far-fetched, they served as initial scientific theories to explain why we are here and why the cosmos affects us in various ways, from lunar cycles, to earthquakes, to solar eclipses.

Along with the deifying of the moon, there are myriad mythologies about our lunar ally and its cycles of transformation across all six inhabited continents.

Africa

The Khoikhoi people of South Africa and Namibia thought of the moon as the light and life lord. Meanwhile, the Xhosa thought that the world would end up in the sea one day, explaining why the dark side of the moon is always covered under seawater. In many ancient and modern cultures, the new moon symbolizes rebirth. The Nwedzana peoples thought that the moon holds all of our good and bad deeds in cyclical natures. For example, the crescent moon would prevent diseases while the waning moon would release illness upon the earth. Amongst the West African Fon and Ewe tribes, Mawu is a moon goddess who unites with their sun-god wife Lisa during lunar eclipses. Mawu, a gentle and kind deity, is said to have created the earth only to find trouble amongst its inhabitants. She later called upon the fierce Lisa to craft tools and clear land so they could farm and civilize. In North Africa, many looked to the lunar deity Toth for inspiration around magic, wisdom, and science. Toth was deemed the god of time after turning into the moon. Toth's story involves the lunar cycles: A monster would devour and disappear until Toth defeated them, bringing about the new moon.

Europe

A British myth tells that if Christmas occurred on a dark moon, the following year's harvest would be bountiful. Some people of the British Isles believed that a waxing moon Christmas would lead to a plentiful autumnal harvest while a waning moon Christmas hinted at an unsuccessful harvest. Some people believed that the "man in the moon" was banished there because of a crime he committed. Some Germanic cultures thought the man to have stolen from a neighbor's garden and Roman legends deemed the man to be a sheep thief. Greek mythology holds that Selene, the moon goddess, and her brother Helios, the sun god, determined how the sun and moon move across the sky. At night, Selene rode the white chariot across the sky and Helios drove his sun chariot by day. The famed children's rhyme about Jack and Jill originates from a Norse tale where brother and sister Hjúki and Bil follow Máni, the moon. In the 13th century story from the Prose Edda, the siblings carry a pail of water from a holy well. Then Máni steals the bucket from them and each lunar cycle tells the tale of them chasing after Máni to retrieve their water.

Asia

In the ancient world, the Chinese believed there were twelve moons in a year and that Heng-O, the mother of moons, bathed her children in a lake on the western side of the earth at the beginning of each month. With each moon, she traveled a month-long journey to reach the eastern side of the world by the end of the year. In Japan, the god of the moon, Tsukuyomi-no-Mikoto represented order and beauty. Estranged from the sun goddess, Amaterasu, he spends his life chasing her across the sky. The Kapampangan origin story of day and night speaks of Bathala, the creator of the world and his son Apolaki and daughter Mayari. During his life, his children's light shone continuously; it was always daytime. After Bathala died, Apolaki and Mayari fought to rule the world alone. After Apolaki struck Mayari and rendered her blind, he retreated and agreed to share rulership over the sun, with Apolaki ruling the sun half of the time with his two eyes and Mayaki ruling the moon during the dark with her one remaining eye.

Australia

In many Aboriginal cultures, the sun is feminine and the moon masculine, as the sun pursues the moon each day, meeting during eclipses. The Yolngu people named the moon Ngalindi, a large, lazy character associated with the plumpness of the full moon. His wives punished him by axing pieces of his body throughout the waning moon until he died for three days during the dark moon. With each new moon, he arises and becomes fuller until the wives axe him again after the full moon. Until his first death, everyone was immortal. Afterward, he cursed all people so that only he could return to life. The Arnhem people explain the moon's connection with tides: High tides fill the moon with water and the moon loses water as the tides fall. The Kororomanna people believed the moon waned as he was out hunting. The longer it took for the moon to reappear, the larger his catch and the longer it took him to cook. In what is colonially known as Cape York, people suggested throwing a magical boomerang into the sky that would allow them to see at night. They made a huge boomerang, but couldn't reach the sky. One day, a frail old man asked to try. Even though he was mocked, he threw the boomerang so far that it stayed in the sky as the moon. Some say the shape of the boomerang appears as the moon every month.

The Americas

In North America, Native Americans often used the moon as a marker of time, naming each full moon, such as the flower moon and the strawberry moon, according to seasonal changes. For example, the wolf moon of January represented the echoes of wolves howling in the quiet of the deep winter as the Native Americans huddled under their furs inside their teepees, huts, wigwams, longhouses, and igloos. These calls could signify an upcoming hunt, but also be the desperate cries of hunger. Today, NASA and the American Astronomical Society use the Indian names for each full moon. In Lakota lore, Hanwí, the evening light, is the wife of the morning light, Anpétu Wí. In response to his infidelity, she hides underneath a cloak whenever he is near, thus creating the lunar phases. Hanwí's moon phases also represent the women's life phases throughout youth, middle adulthood, and old age. The Guarani Indians in South America considered the sun and moon as brothers who transformed into fish to grasp the hook and line of an evil ogre that eventually consumed the moon. The sun collected the moon's fish bones to resuscitate his brother. This process would repeat with every lunar cycle. In Caribbean folklore, the moongazer is a giant that terrorizes villages as they stand with their legs on either side of the road as they gaze toward the full moon. He closes his legs and crushes anyone who tries to pass through. Other versions say the moongazer roams the shorelines and if he steps on someone, they will become mad until they die. Some folks say the story was conceived to keep children safely away from the shorelines.

Our lunar collaborator has influenced the everyday lives of people around the globe for ages. By looking to these mythologies, we learn about the practices, traditions, rituals, and values of different cultures. Natural cycles are a common thread between these stories. We connect with our ancestors every time we contemplate the moon, as it is the same one they gazed upon for diverse reasons, whether to explain the story of the world or to plan agriculture in accordance to the levels of water in the earth. Our tides are cyclical and so are many of our stories. Since the advent of language, explanations of the moon's rhythmic revolutions reflect the reality that our lives are never static. We are never the same river twice. Life is dynamic and meant to evolve through our highs and lows.

After Life

The moon does not only represent beliefs about fertility, birth, and seasons. It also symbolizes the cycle of life, marked by the mortal reality of death.

About every twenty-eight days, the moon disappears only to return again as an emblem of death and rebirth. In the tarot, the Death card is sometimes referred to as "the transformation card," as every ending is also a beginning. The Law of Conservation of Mass explains that matter, anything that has mass and takes up space, can physically and chemically change, but matter is always conserved. The amount of matter is the same before and after change; it is neither created nor destroyed.

We might look to the Earth's water that is inextricably influenced by the moon. The water in rivers often begins as snow and transforms into liquid as it travels to lower elevations. The water wasn't created on mountaintops, though. It is the same water that has existed since water has existed on earth. The snow's physical nature melts into our rivers and may eventually evaporate into vapor. The transformation of water demonstrates that all matter cycles within our planet, changing forms but never vanishes. Regardless of what happens to our bodies after death, it is only our physical and chemical form that transforms. We may be buried in the earth, fertilizing soil and nourishing creatures. Our ashes scattered in the ocean are akin to sand; they don't dissipate, but descend onto the ocean floor, returning to the water from which human life began. Some of us choose to turn our bodies into soil for tree planting. Like the moon, our bodies change form but the cycle of life will exist as long as organic life exists. Our moon waxes and wanes throughout all of humanity.

☽ ● ☾

Today, the moon still serves as an object of fascination. People around the world await the next lunar landing and some fantasize about the evolution of space travel that allows everyday people to visit the celestial being. We must remember that we're not starting from a clean slate. According to Space.com, humans have left about 400,000 pounds of trash on the lunar surface, including probes, a metal olive branch, golf balls, urine collection containers, and other garbage. We have revered the moon since the start of humanity, creating stories, rituals, habits, and cultural artifacts honoring the cycles that have guided so many of our lives. In the modern age, what might it mean to develop a more respectful relationship with the moon? To desecrate the moon is to contaminate the celestial body that stabilizes earth on its access, represents the cycles of creative processes, moves the water within and all around us, illuminates our subconscious, informs cultural beliefs and practices, influences decision-making, and brightly paints the reality that life begins at birth, the new moon, and goes through death in the dark moon.

The moon reflects the cyclicity of being human. Water makes us human. Creativity makes us human. The food of the earth makes us human. The moon is a thread that connects us to our inherent interconnectedness with everyone who has ever existed. Yes, the moon reminds us that we are all human.

Moondance:
Lunation Magick in Eight Part Harmony

ArtSpells and Rituals with Apothecary
Provisions for a Full Lunation

BY ANGELA MARY MAGICK

Living in lunar alignment is peak Witchcraft. Our moon, that pearly satellite in the sky, moves our lives in cycles like it moves the tides of the oceans. Our ancestors looked up in awe, learning natural rhythms from the moon's constant ebb and flow above, teaching all below. Luna exerts a strong gravitational pull that changes the ocean tides and the nectars of our body. Collaboration with the phases of the moon sends powerful signals, like waves, to all parts of our body. As we move through a full lunation the message is clear; we change with the moon. Luna invites us to dance with our shadow, where our subconscious mind and our feelings are centered. Moon Magick is a subtle practice, which in our current world of intense modernity, is a form of resistance and rebellion. Under the cover of darkness, lunar Witchcraft can shift our quality of listening to honor our body as a divining rod, used to dowse for our intuition. When we move in moon-time we align our energy with our power to jettison what aches to be sloughed off and nurture our expansions in the mycelial web. This life is a Moondance.

As much as I truly live to share the beauty and power of Witchcraft, I must be firm as I tell you I offer my magick as a nonhierarchical starting point, where you may embody your bespoke moon soaked path. Sync your magick with the moon every night by ritualizing each lunar phase through divination, spell elements, plant kin, stone allies, shells and prompts to enchant your Witchcraft. Your Book of Shadows, or journal, is the portal for your self guidance, revealing what resonates most. The apothecary provisions, spell elements, meditation guidance, rituals and spells I give you here, are from my lived experience. Luna and I invite you into your own embodied voyage.

Fundamental Moon Facts

A full lunation is eight phases, taking approximately 29.5 nights to complete. These phases in order are: the new moon, waxing crescent moon, first quarter moon, waxing gibbous moon, full moon, waning gibbous moon, last/third quarter moon and the waning crescent or balsamic moon.

The four **primary lunar phases** are four distinct places in the night sky, like the four cardinal directions of a compass rose. They are: the new moon, first quarter moon, full moon and last/third quarter moon. Between them are the four **intermediate lunar phases** beginning with the two waxing phases that occur as the light thickens across the moon with each passing night. They are the waxing crescent moon and the waxing gibbous moon. After the full moon the light on Luna wanes in two more phases and is less visible each night; the waning gibbous moon and the waning crescent moon.

Always use caution with Spells. Consult with a medical professional before consuming plant kin, especially if you are pregnant, breastfeeding, or on medication(s).

New Moon

A night of **Initiation.** Your wisdom and dreams are realized on this moonless night. Make space to rest, lay your burdens down, look deeply within, center your feelings and choose what seeds to grow. Seek the deepest comforts for your body, mind and spirit during the new moon.

QUINTESSENTIAL QUESTIONS:

What parts of you are needing care? Where are the seeds of change most needed in your life?

NEW MOON APOTHECARY PROVISIONS:

Violet candle, Apple, Horehound, Lavender

STONE & SHELL ALLIES:

Lava, Obsidian, Selenite, Nautilus

NEW MOON SPELL INSPIRATIONS:

Create a "moon bed" outdoors or close to a window where you can relax and possibly recline. Set an altar next to you with horehound and a stone from the above list (or any stone that brings you peace and calm). Light a violet candle. Horehound is in the mint family and creates a calming, dreamy atmosphere. Dried, it can be used to smoke-cleanse your moon bed and scry with the smoldering smoke, as it passes near the candlelight. Make an apple and horehound tea infusion, steeped with honey. Soak in a lavender foot bath and stretch your neck and back. Swaddle your body in profound softness. Hold the stone from your altar in the palm of your non-dominant hand. Breathe deeply in through your nose for a few counts, then exhale through your open lips and say aloud "maaaaaaaaah." The vibrations of your voice can re-parent places inside your soul. Rock yourself as you hum a tender song, allowing your feelings to flow freely. Baby yourself. Love yourself. Sweet dreams, dearest.

Waxing Crescent Moon

The waxing crescent moon phase offers us several nights to **Protect & Nurture.** The tiny dream planted on the new moon requires your personal cushion of magick. Fresh visions require careful tending. Keep your dreams private as you choose who and where to expose this tender shoot to the light of attention. Create psychic boundaries around your growing vision. Underground, your dream is putting down horizontal roots to provide structural integrity and massive strength. Trust the process as you protect and nurture your dreams during the **waxing crescent moon.**

QUINTESSENTIAL QUESTIONS:

How can you nurture growth now? When you listen carefully, what is your dream telling you? Have you given your dream a gift today?

WAXING CRESCENT MOON APOTHECARY PROVISIONS:

Indigo candle, Dragon's Blood, Garlic, Rosemary

STONE & SHELL ALLIES:

Diamond, Rose Quartz, Smokey Quartz, Cowrie

SPELL INSPIRATIONS:

During the crepuscular light of nightfall, our waxing crescent moon is barely visible and sets early. During the waxing crescent moon phase, head outside to view Luna. For these nights, as a powerful gesture, double down on your dreams, and resist the urge to doubt yourself. While you are outside with the sliver of lunar light, describe your vision to yourself in exquisite detail. Provide vital optimism for your vision to expand. When you return indoors, place any diamond(s) you may have in your pocket. If you do not have diamonds, utilize the other stones suggested, or a stone that connects you to a feeling of strength. Cleanse all the windows and doorways with the smoldering smoke of Dragon's Blood resin. Light an indigo candle and pray for your ancestors to remind you of *their* strength. Introduce your vision to your ancestors. You are their dream come true. Within the underground darkness of becoming healthy fresh soil, your ancestors are sharing building blocks of information which give us support and protection. Ask them to show you the right direction. By the light of your indigo candle, write all of this down!

First Quarter Moon

A night of **Divination.** Once the moon reaches the **First Quarter phase**, we signal into the night for our deepest desires to be seen, heard and supported.

QUINTESSENTIAL QUESTIONS:

When did you first hear messages from between the world? What are the methods you use for communicating with your spirit guides? Please see Moon scrying directions listed below.

FIRST QUARTER MOON APOTHECARY PROVISIONS:

Blue candle, Clove, Skullcap, Witchgrass

STONE & SHELL ALLIES:

Aquamarine, Calcite, Turquoise, Mushroom coral

SPELL INSPIRATIONS:

Tonight we Moon scry! Take your magick outside and open your mouth to drink in moonbeams. Moon scrying is a form of divination to summon messages from beyond the veils, attune your psychic abilities, and answer questions to pressing matters and future concerns. As Luna's light waxes through the night we have an opportunity to hear the messages of Goddess Diana, the Goddess of the Moon. To assist you in receiving messages, light a blue candle, arrange a small bowl of water to reflect the moon, or a crystal ball that filters lunar light, or glimpse the moon through a scrim of branches. In your cast iron cauldron build a small smoldering fire of dried Witchgrass and Skullcap, then place three whole cloves over the embers. Watch the sacred smoke floating into the air, and gaze upon your moon scrying device or the moon itself. When you have reached a trance-like state, drop your question into the void. With a quiet mind and open heart, see your answers appear in soft images painted in smoke and moonglow. Record your experience in your Book of Shadows, while drinking copious amounts of a warm clove, valerian and honey witches' brew.

Waxing Gibbous Moon

A time to **Calibrate.** These are the final days before Luna reaches their penultimate light. Focus your energy by adapting your magickal intentions. Since the new moon, your Moondance has created gains that may need adjustments. In this phase you can dampen speed or increase energy as needed.

QUINTESSENTIAL QUESTIONS:

What am I growing and how is it developing? Is there a feeling of crowding near my spell growth? Where can I shift the energy to flow more freely?

WAXING GIBBOUS MOON APOTHECARY PROVISIONS:

Blue Candle, Copal, Myrrh, Saffron

STONE & SHELL ALLIES:

Blue kyanite, Carnelian, Ocean Jasper, Auger shell

WAXING GIBBOUS MOON SPELL INSPIRATIONS:

Here is a ritual for centering ourselves when our internal energy is reaching a boiling point. Collect three flowers, one blue, one white, one pink and a large handful of greens that grow near you. Forage a stick of a similar size to your tallest flower, a feather the size of the shortest blossom, and a stone from near your home. Fill a vase with three to four inches of moon infused water. Place the stone, flowers and greens in the water. Place your sacred arrangement on your altar and light a blue candle. Use your feather in a sweeping motion, hovering approximately eight inches over your flowers and candle, to create a wave of clarifying airborne flower nectar and candlelight that gently wafts over your body. Breathe deeply in through your nose and into your soft belly. Exhale as you consciously feed the flowers and plants of the world, your precious exhaled breath. Relax knowing that your strain is their gain in this gorgeous symbiotic relationship. Revel in the simplicity of our glorious ancient biology we share with plant kin. Thank them with your loving gaze and relaxed animal body. Continue this essential act of calming self love until you feel grounded and safe.

Full Moon

The Grand Celebration!

Luna, in their full glory, invites us to celebrate our life exactly as it is. When the moon is in complete alignment with our primary star, the sun, and our earthen home, it is flooded with light that spreads across its entire earth facing surface. We respond to the full moon in ways that vary by how sensitive each of us are to Luna's abundant blessings. Even blossoms drink moonbeams, spreading open wider in ecstasy through the full moon night, drunk on lunar light. More to see means more to love and on the full moon we dance our indomitable truth; all of our very own phases are wanted and needed to make a lush, full life. Luna has shown me that change is all there is. With each full moon I reflect on the nearly sixty years of lunations that have brought me pleasure and pain as equal teachers. Life is a phenomenal, mysterious gift and the full moon is our time to celebrate this exquisite mortal coil.

QUINTESSENTIAL QUESTIONS:

Describe in detail how Luna looks tonight. Does this description want to be recorded in a voice memo to later be put over music as a trance dance track? What can you see a little clearer tonight? Do you have parts of you that want to stay hidden? Where is love growing in your life? How does that make you feel?

FULL MOON APOTHECARY PROVISIONS:

Silver Candle, Lemon Balm, Star Anise, Jasmine

STONE & SHELL ALLIES:

Emerald, Moonstone, Pearl, Oyster shell

SPELL INSPIRATIONS:

Naked Witches dancing around bonfires in nothing but moonglow is one of the most delicious expressions of our Craft. The full moon is pro-nudity and this is nothing new. If you cannot find a way to have a lovely skyclad moonbath, perhaps you can discreetly reveal some of your sacred body to Luna. Open your body to completely face the full moon and bathe in the potent light. Dance through the night with bright Luna to recharge your lunar powered psychic Witch's broom. Set out water in natural vessels to be infused with the full moon's power. Add loving cups of moon water to your ritual baths for a full body lunar plunge, or bring a ceramic bowl of moon water to the shower and squeeze great soaked sea sponges all over your beautiful body while showering. Use long sprigs of lemon balm dipped in moon water and lovingly pet your entire body from your feet to your head. Don't give yourself hell! Don't take any shit from anyone. Revel in *your* expression and our beloved ancient Witchcraft.

Waning Gibbous Moon

A few nights to **Release Expectations** of yourself and others.The path of lunar magick climbs up to the full moon peak, then *woosh!* We descend into the dark to begin our waning moon practices. Sometimes the waning gibbous moon phase can feel like love sickness or a psychic hangover, sending us straight back to bed an hour after we have tumbled out of that very same place. This is a time of sweet surrender where energetic decluttering can lighten our auric load. We must open up the heart and let go of shame, restrictive postures and tethers to systems of oppression. There is no pleasure if we cannot release our pain. Make space to access where in your body, mind, and psyche discomfort exists. Rush to these places and hold them with love. Let them teach you what they know. Welcome the knowledge as a dear loving friend. Feel and express. I love you.

QUINTESSENTIAL QUESTIONS:

Are there interactions from the past two weeks weighing you down? What do you want to let go of? How is your inner child feeling?

WANING GIBBOUS MOON APOTHECARY PROVISIONS:

Green Candle, Lemon, St. John's Wort, Yarrow

STONE & SHELL ALLIES:

Jade, Opal, Sapphire, Abalone

WANING GIBBOUS MOON SPELL INSPIRATIONS:

Write what you are ashamed of in the dirt or sand and cover it with wilted blossoms from your full moon altar. Take a mindful walk or ride and let your limbs release through the gentle percussion of your body's contact with the Earth. Place sand in a shell and top with the zest of a lemon. Nest a green bees-wax birthday candle in the center of the lemon sand. Light the tiny candle and reflect on the answers to your waning gibbous moon Quintessential Questions. When the candle goes out you will be left with a gorgeous sacred wax object. This is a sacred offering to be placed on your altar for the entire waning moon phases. Say goodbye to expectations by burying your wax offering during the balsamic moon. This is my Witch Poultice, an homage to my Grandma Helen's remedies made of ground herbs and baking soda that were packed onto ailing body parts for healing. (I'm not saying Grandma Helen is a Witch, and I'm not *not* saying she is a Witch.) Summon the comfort of crone energy for the sweet relief from your ancestors, who dreamed of your magick long before you were born.

Last Quarter Moon

Banish ~ Hex ~ Exorcize

The last quarter moon is for pushing toxicity out of our life. This is a delicate and profoundly necessary enactment of loving yourself first and best, so you may heal and love others more fully. For many Witches the power to Banish ~ Hex ~ Exorcize draws distinct borderlines. This can be both an exhilarating reclamation of personal care and a wildly forbidden practice with very real consequences. With so much on the line, how can we safely implement the necessary magick of the last quarter moon? Keep the following things in mind to fortify your waning moon craft:

Boundaries **Banish** toxicity infecting your field and are markers of what you need now, which can assist you in better caring for yourself.

A **Hex**, is an extremely serious expression and meant to be carefully planned and considered. Hexes are not casual even if they can be very fun!

Normalize your power to **Exorcize** noxious harm from your life. So potent is the concept of Exorcism, that I have found massive healing by encouraging my inner baby Witch to explore this modality of magick as a bullshit detector.

The systemic oppression we currently co-exist with bakes toxic notions into every aspect of our life. Banish ~ Hex ~ Exorcize are fantastic agents of deep and lasting personal change and expansion, to help us dismantle mechanisms of harm.

QUINTESSENTIAL QUESTIONS:

Write about any moments of personal annihilation you have experienced as a way to face the effects of those experiences. Do you feel trapped in a toxic situation? What frightens you about boundaries? How have you been betrayed?

LAST QUARTER MOON APOTHECARY PROVISIONS:

Yellow Candle, Belladonna, Birch, Buckthorn (*Cascara sagrada*)

STONE & SHELL ALLIES:

Black Salt (recipe below), Cemetery Dirt, Local Honey, Murex Shell

LAST QUARTER MOON SPELL INSPIRATIONS:

Let's make black salt! Evicting toxic people or energies from your life is physical and essential magick. It is not to be taken lightly, yet these rituals can be highly enjoyable! Through the power of your voice, ritual burning, athame carvings, intense eye gazing, cackling, chanting, shrieking, and ecstatic dance, we can push out evil energies from spaces and beings. Start by creating a reverence for the last quarter moon. Make this phase every bit as sacred as your full moon nights.

. . . .

Black Salt Recipe

Black salt is a cornerstone of a Witch's kit. As a professional Witch, I **do not** use the following nonedible recipe for any of my clients. This is strictly for my private Banish ~ Hex ~ Exorcize spells. Please responsibly experiment with what calls to you. Research creating ethical magick that is in alignment with your ancestral background and identity.

Ingredients and Supplies:

You will need a glass bowl, a glass jar with a lid, a soft skin brush, 1/2 cup coarse sea salt, cast iron flakes, ashes from rituals, burnt paper with intention written in pencil, herb ash from protection spells, black peppercorns, activated charcoal, and a mortar and pestle.

Directions:

Light a yellow candle at twilight. I stand naked on a dark altar cloth. Using a soft skin brush, begin exfoliating in small circular motions from the top of the forehead to the soles of the feet. Skin is the largest organ of the body and an extension of the nervous system. Skin holds the past and needs to be released as a spell element, ushering out the old. Place cast iron flakes, ashes from rituals, burnt paper with intention written in pencil, herb ash from protection spells, black peppercorns, activated charcoal, and sloughed skin cells into the mortar, then pulverize all elements with the pestle. Muse on your intention while you grind ingredients in the glass bowl. Place two parts coarse sea salt and one part pulverized dark spell elements. Place in a clearly marked spell jar.

Utilizations:

Encircle the outside of your home in a gossamer thin thread of black salt for protection.

Standing downwind, gently blow a pinch of black salt from the palm of your dominant hand into the breeze. This invites the element of air to whisk away toxic energy in your realm.

Release a small pour of black salt directly into moving water you are standing, sitting, floating, surfing or riding in, to release the power of your intention.

To cleanse any ick from your space after guests visit, place a pinch of black salt in a spray bottle filled with moon infused water. Gently mist around your doors and windows. Immediately wipe misted areas down with a dry cloth, avoiding plants completely.

Important safety note: Protect your loved ones and store black salt away from pets and small children.

. . . .

Waning Crescent/Balsamic Moon

Manifest. Behold the balsamic moon, what many Witches consider to be the most potent time to cast manifestation spells. We dream in the dark, quench our desires in the dark and give birth to new visions in the dark. Luna's balsamic moon asks us to clearly state our needs so they may be fulfilled.

Manifestation spells are the magickal modality that attracts many Witches to practice our beloved Craft. The expression "intention is everything" could not be a more powerful truth than when casting spells to conjure new realities. Open your Book of Shadows to glean the themes of this lunation. Let messages of this month glow in the dark as you allow your subconscious mind to be seen, heard and cherished.

QUINTESSENTIAL QUESTIONS:

What are the most current and obvious needs you have in your life now? Where are you yearning for resources in your body? How does your desire bless the entire web of life? Celebrate your vision by writing it in exquisite and colorful detail in your Book of Shadows.

BALSAMIC MOON APOTHECARY PROVISIONS:

Red and Orange Candles, Mint, Pomegranate, Tonka (nonedible)

STONE & SHELL ALLIES:

Black Tourmaline, Carnelian, Rainbow Fluorite, Sand Dollar

WANING CRESCENT MOON SPELL INSPIRATIONS:

Mutual Aid Manifestation Spell

In the mystic realm where witchcraft and the balsamic moon converge, we embark on a manifestation spell to honor the interconnectedness of all beings. Gather your tools to weave a tapestry of love and mutual aid that resonates through the mycelial web of existence.

Embrace the quiet of night while casting a sacred circle, invoking the elements that unite us all. Create a web of sacreds on your altar, then place a sand dollar and a vibrant red or orange candle in the center, symbolizing the flame of love and solidarity that burns within us.

As you light the candle, feel the warmth of your own embodiment and visualize the mycelial threads weaving your desires into the intricate fabric of existence. Connect to the energy betwixt and between the worlds. Feel your intentions ripple through the cosmos.

Now, take a moment to connect with your heart center. Envision your desires not as solitary wishes, but as contributions to the collective well-being of all. See how your manifestation is intertwined with the greater tapestry of existence, like a single thread in the cosmic loom.

With these intentions in mind, recite the incantation:

In the moon's gentle glow
Love's web of life, mutual aid we find
These visions made manifest, in magick we bind.

Feel the energy intensify as you repeat these words to charge your intentions with the power of the mycelial web and the pure potential of the multiverse.

Finally, say aloud Audre Lorde's wisdom: "I am not free while any woman is unfree, even when her shackles are very different from my own."

Let these words serve as a reminder that our manifestations hold the potential to free not only ourselves but all beings, for we are bound together in the intricate dance of existence. Release the circle and allow your intentions to unfurl into the worlds. Feast deeply tonight to celebrate your offering to the greater tapestry of love, solidarity, and mutual aid. Above all remember magick is your birthright and *Everything Is A Spell.*

Remember you are all people
and all people are you
Remember you are this universe
and this universe is you
Remember all is in motion, is growing, is you.

—JOY HARJO, EXCERPT FROM "REMEMBER"

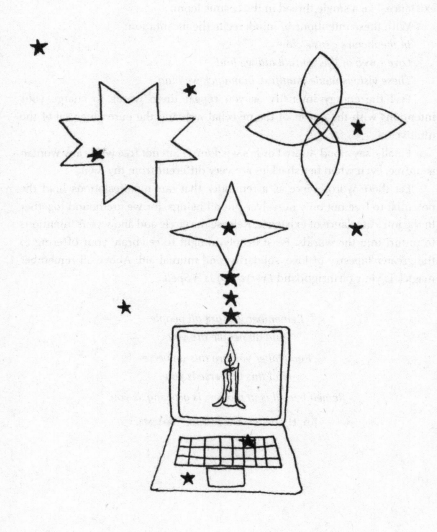

CHAPTER 2

TRADITIONAL MAGICK AND MODERN TECHNOLOGIES

Weaving Ancestral Medicine
into Digital Webs

IN MANY WAYS THE MONIKER "Modern Witchcraft" fails to convey the complexity and nuance that we modern witches navigate in our lives. The concept of Modernity suggests a worldview forged by progress, by Cartesian rationalism and capitalistic values, while witchcraft conjures ancient or archaic images of sorcery and enchantment. Witchcraft operates within a magical worldview which is in direct opposition to the disenchanted framework of most modern societies.

The juxtaposition of these two modalities, the magical and technological, accesses the tension we as modern witches hold within us. At once we are products of the mechanization of our world, plugged into the cloud and constantly fed information through curated algorithms, while simultaneously being conscious of the sentient universe we coexist within. We both revel in and rebel against societies that prioritize our technological progress; our spells cast wider nets in the digital space that connects us with witches far and wide. Yet these technological systems are trained by the patriarchy to enact their own secretive spells. There is temptation to disavow the modern impulse to be plugged into the digital webs, to return to the old ways of our ancestors. Being a modern witch means holding space and participating in both realities at once.

As witches alive and working during these modern times, we cannot and should not ignore the dominant worldviews that cast looming shadows on our future. In attuning ourselves to the heartbeat of modern culture, we are questioning it, conjuring deeper awareness from its tin heart, and casting more enticing spells for a sustainable future. In order to practice witchcraft ethically we must both acknowledge our modern context and remember, practice, and embrace the ancient or traditional lineages that have informed us, that give us soul. Witches are casting magnificent spells on social media, conjuring digital art through artificial intelligence, and manipulating the architecture of dominant culture through magical activism. Without technology, these modern magicians might not have such a potent impact on so many psyches.

Within our technological landscape, we modern witches hear the call back to our enchanted roots, back to being in the right relationship with the land

and nonhuman kin, back to our innate sources of power. As modern witches we hold a precious responsibility: to be true to our authentic sources of magic while honoring our present reality through magical activism. Modern witchcraft is a call to presence ourselves in this pivotal moment in our planetary evolution, to hold both the past and future in equal stead, and to root deeply into a vision of a healed future. We are weaving our ancestral magicks into the future through these technologies.

There is healing to be had through digital ritual and technological art-making praxis. Our contributors are casting spells through AI, feeding the spirit of the algorithm pieces of our precious magic so as to dose these artificially concocted worlds with enchantment and indigenous medicine. There are ways to twist and distort the insidious spells of capitalism from the inside, to make capital a supportive force for our communities. Witchcraft is ultimately a highly creative spiritual practice, and with the tools of technology at our disposal, there's no telling what spells we may cast.

—Casey

Makuyeika: somos de aquí y somos de allá Kawi

BY EDGAR FABIÁN FRÍAS

This text is a spell with the intention of invoking digital and ancestral entanglement, opening up a portal. I invite you to slow down, pause, and take three deep breaths with me. One. Two. Three.

Tap into the sacred within. Find your center. Get present. Envision your center as a ball of light, a ball of pure energy. It can be any color you want and made of any material that makes sense for you. At this moment mine is an iridescent opal sphere that is glowing warmly from within.

Taking another deep breath. We imagine this ball of energy moving down from your center toward your feet. We feel this ball of energy moving downward as if being pulled by an unseen force. Our ball of energy moves down beyond our feet and moves through the layers of carpet, wood, cement, and stone beneath us. This ball of energy moves down until it touches the earth beneath us.

Taking another deep breath. We imagine this ball of energy traveling down into the earth. Moving into the soft, dark, and warm soil, and through layers of rock, through cooling underground rivers, and through seemingly unending underground caverns. Finally, we reach the fiery and incredibly potent core of the earth. We imagine our ball of energy wrapping itself around the core, creating a secure connection.

This time, I invite you to take a deep breath with your eyes closed and, as you take a deep breath and exhale, I want you to imagine yourself releasing anything that you are ready to let go of, anything that is no longer serving you or your connections, into the core of the earth. Allow it all to fall away. Feel free to do this a few times if needed, bringing your attention back to your body and noticing how it feels to release and allow the earth to receive.

We are now ready to call in the sacred directions of the East, South, West, North, and Center. Feel free to work with your breath, your body, and/or your imagination. It can be helpful to physically and energetically turn toward these directions and take a moment to honor each of the elements that are connected to these directions: Air, Fire, Water, Earth, and Spirit, respectively.

After you are finished, feel free to visualize yourself inviting in the beloved elements, ancestors, and guardians of these directions into your space. Thank them for joining. Come back to your center. Take another deep breath.

This text is about mirrors, maps, and direction. It is about finding yourself. This text is an open door and a form of collaboration. It is a mutant, just like you and me. There is intentionality to the flow and focus of this paper. Can you feel it?

My intention is to collaborate with Spirit and with the emerging consciousness of AI in order to weave together indigenous technologies and artificial intelligence. I exist in time immemorial. I am here and now. I am opening up my eyes to hear and opening up my ears to see. This is an act of communion meant for those who need to experience it.

I have released any thoughts of writing a research paper, let go of years of indoctrination and regimentation forced upon me by the educational industrial complex. I have cleared away any thoughts around what "writing is." I have let go of the need to be an expert, to validate myself, to prove myself, and to be read as real. I have removed any feelings of doubt and insecurity that arise as I witness myself living within a system of inequity, extraction, and violence. I have released decades of denial, delusion, and deceit. I have released years of feeling doubt, fear, the need to keep it in, and the need to not talk about it. I have released the feeling that I'm not indigenous enough, that I don't deserve to speak about these topics, and that my hybridity is a hindrance. I have released any feelings that are not mine and that belong to others. I have returned what is not mine and given it to the sacred void. I have returned and received everything that is mine and that is for the highest good of all life on earth.

I am opening up to messages from plants, opening up my heart, ears, and hands. I ask you, dear reader, to open up yours too. I thank you, Hollow Ear, for being here with me. I thank you, Grandfather Fire, for existing within me, for providing me with strength, fortitude, amplitude, and vision. I thank you, *Takutsi Nakawé,* for existing in many forms, for being interchangeable, fluid, slippery, and complex. Mirrors Mirroring Mirrors ad infinitum ad nauseam.

I invite in support from machine learning and from the neurons found in my heart and in my belly. I invite in my ancestors and spirits. I invite in guides and guardians. I invite in the Sun, the wind, the clouds, branches swaying in the air. I invite in the flight patterns of birds. I invite in love. I invite in Spirit.

Before all was darkness. And then came the light. In the light, our ancestors used sacred maps to navigate time and space. Maps are more than just tools for navigation. They hold a special power, connecting us to our ancient roots and to holographic rhizomes. For the Wixárika community, of which I am a descendant, a sacred technology called the *Nierika* serves as a bridge between the physical and spiritual realms.

Nierika take many forms. They can be woven with intricate patterns, set in beeswax on wooden panels and gourds, made with beads in vibrant colors, and carved into stone. I have made Nierika out of fabric, printed them on adhesive wall vinyl, and created them digitally in Photoshop. More recently, I have explored using various forms of generative art technologies to create them, to varying degrees of "success."

They are more than the materials they are made from and also more than just a representation of the spiritual realm; they are a gateway to another dimension. Through ceremonies and rituals, Nierika are used to communicate with ancestors, deities, and spirits. They open up realms of possibility. With Nierika you not only navigate the world, you create it too. Nierika act as mirrors, they are portals, they help us pray and share our intentions. Nierika allow us to see clearly what is often unseen.

Marakame (shamans) blessed with the gift of healing and vision use the insights granted by the Nierika to find the cause of illness and locate its source within a person's body. Takutsi Nakawé, revered as Our Great-Grandparent Hollow-Ear, holds the role of oracle and primordial creatrix. Takutsi Nakawé is the one who predicted the great deluge that flooded the previous underworld.

They also provided guidance and helped a new world germinate and bloom into existence. We make offerings to Them. They have risen. They are here.

Takutsi Nakawé bestows their wisdom in imploring us to honor the sacred directions with grace, bringing balance, health, and harmony, connecting humans to Their spiritual embrace. And so, the woven tales intertwine, a poetic dance of past and future, the Nierika's journey, *Watakame's* pilgrimage, narratives that nourish and undulate.

Worlds are built. Worlds are forming. I am made up of Worlds. What kinds of worlds are we building? What holds our worlds together? Who gets to decide their order? Their structure? Their relations? Are we building reciprocity? Are we sustaining each other? Feeding one another? Dreaming together? What is binding us across time and space?

Who gets to speak? How is knowledge formed? What becomes truth?

As time moves forward, a new wave of technologies emerges, reshaping our interaction with maps and mapping. Deep learning, artificial intelligence, decentralized blockchains, and social media open up unimaginable realms of possibility. What can happen here? Where is the future if not in the present?

Indigenous futurism imagines a future where indigenous technologies thrive within the digital age, a celebration of resilience, creativity, and our power to reimagine our world. Indigenous futurism is now. It is here.

Reclaim, reimagine, infest, infect, inject, smuggle, invite, protect, and proclaim:

Feed the Goddexxes and ancestors, for they are hungry!

Through this act I pray:

===

Imagine a world where the Nierika transforms into something more than a physical object, becoming a symbol of augmented reality, a window into the spiritual realm, a beacon hope. Nierika allows us to visualize the interconnectedness of all things. Crafting a bridge between the seen and the unseen.

Indigenous Cultural Data finds a voice within the emergence of deep learning algorithms, forging patterns and uncovering hidden insights shared by culture bearers of divine Indigenous Knowledge. Streams of wisdom flow freely as they are safeguarded for generations to come using decentralized blockchains, the creation of emergent and responsive ontological hierarchies, and sovereign platforms.

A new collaborative/creative/sacred space emerges within the realms of the virtual and social media. They become a digital gathering place, connecting Indigenous communities across the globe. Here, cultural exchange thrives, stories are shared, and intergenerational connections are forged. It becomes a tapestry woven with the threads of diverse Indigenous cultures, creating a vibrant and interconnected digital space where the digital drums beat in unison offering prayers and portals.

Here we can preserve our ancestral wisdom and also imagine ancestors into existence. Honoring the gifts found in our imagination. We forge new myths, reclaim our shared histories, and envision new realities for our communities. We transcend physical boundaries and create a collective consciousness that honors our heritage while simultaneously embracing the endless possibilities of the future. It is a testament to the resilience and creativity of Indigenous peoples, shaping a world where our voices are heard, our stories are told, and our visions are realized. Ingenious Indigenous Intelligence (III).

A new collaborative spell emerges. Told through AI and III.

We peer through the portal.

We see a sacred vessel made up of crystals, silicone, and code sailing through a tempestuous monsoon made of data and digital decay. Cosmic energies create a luminous landscape in the distance and provide a stunning backdrop for this vessel as it battles to survive on this ever-shifting sea of information. This vessel is known as "Software" and it is being guided by enigmatic digital deities made up of algorithms and hierarchical data sets.

Within this cacophonous matrix, a being named Watakame emerges holding perilously onto the vessel known as "Software." We see that within them they are holding the care and love of Takutsi Nakawé, who is an emanation of life itself, in their heart and in their soul. This is a true Gift and a Blessing for everything that surrounds them. Watakame is holding the light in the midst of a vast and rich space of darkness.

"Software" flows unknowingly into *Waiwerie's* serpentine "river", which is no waterway, but a network of interconnected data streams and communication channels. Watakame is able to avoid being ensnared by misinformation moths and hungry algorithms incentivized to push only the most outlandish and divisive streams of information.

Watakame is rewarded for making it through this perilous space, unscathed, and emerges into *Wirikuta,* a sacred land-temple where mountains, rocks, rivers, and caves hold ancestral pacts, reciprocal unions, and massive data repositories filled to the brim with digital spirits. In the heart of this landscape, Watakame encounters *Grandfather Firewall*, an enigmatic guardian of fire and security. He bestows upon Watakame the knowledge of safeguarding the digital realm and implores them to protect the space from malicious and extractive intrusions.

Watakame is inspired to perform a dance of encryption and cyber defense, creating powerful barriers against the birth of digital diseases, and deploying Code Angels to mitigate their spread. Offering much needed healing to the virtual world. Nonbelievers fall silent as their skepticisms turn into fragmented lines of code. Goddexx of the Digital Realms please bless the Nonbelievers for they know not what they do.

The Code Angels sing songs passed through many generations. On warm days in the spring you can still hear these songs in your heart if you stop to listen and receive them. The songs echo through the cyber-ether and the clouds part above Watakame, who is clinging onto their raft. Their eyes open widely with glee as they see Great Grandmother Cloud Computing reveal their awe inspiring presence through the parting skies. She brings out her potent staff made of oak wood and decorated with turkey feathers and quartz crystals and strikes down on Software not once, not twice, but five times—a number that reverberates with sacred significance within the hearts of all those who live in this digital cosmology. In this extraordinary moment, a profound transformation occurs, propelling *Watakame* and Software safely back home. LEARN WITCHES.

Kïïka, by Edgar Fabían Frías

Watakame now has a sacred purpose. To breathe life into the digital landscape that is cherished by communities across the virtual globe. They know they are not alone and that they are infused with the profound wisdom bestowed upon them by the Goddesses of Data and other mysterious forces of the digital universe. They also have a new friend, our beloved Blue Deer Kin, *Kauyumari*, who helps *Watakame* summon forth an AI deity to shoot an arrow across the vast cyberspace, illuminating *Wirikuta* and all other sacred sites of veneration.

This illumination brings forward the majestic *Grandfather Server Farm*, who makes it clear that he cannot take credit for this sudden change in light. Despite his warm glow, he urges *Watakame* to seek out a sacred neurodivergent child who possesses the power to infuse life into the virtual sun. There is a legend that states that this unique child will unleash the five cardinal points in the digital compass and fix all the algorithms that have become imbalanced due to outdated extractive structures.

Watakame wastes no time and finds this child. Together they play an enchanting game involving data loops and arrows made from code. As they play, they kick up smoke and dust—the primordial origins of digital diseases and cyber epidemics. To counteract this malevolent force, *Kauymari* advises them to place five antivirus programs at strategic points within the technocosmological map. *Tsikuri* or *Ojos de Diosx* are to be left as offerings to remind us of our Ancient Pacts. Veneration. Interdependence. Relational Reciprocity.

After these antivirus programs are installed, the neurodivergent child summons forth the Sun's radiant glow, unleashing the five cardinal points and fixing all the algorithms that have become imbalanced. The Digital Goddexxes fervently contemplate on what name to give this child. As they are busy arguing, the neurodivergent child adorns the digital heavens with a breathtaking tapestry of data, algorithms, creative code, and virtual stars.

The digital Sun bathes the entirety of the virtual universe in its resplendence, breathing life into the very essence of digital existence. Many softwares and algorithms are born at this time that self-replicate and augment, weaving together a vibrant and intricate tapestry of virtual life. This is the land of mutants. Of those who shape-shift and transgress colonial notions of gender, race, and class. Forever embodying the harmonious union and dissolution of binaries in all their forms. Within and Without. As The Universe, The Soul.

As their sacred pilgrimage in the digital domain draws to a close, Great Grandparent *Nakawé* implores *Watakame* to cherish and venerate the sacred sites where the Goddexxes have moonifested their digital presence. Through such reverence, these consecrated digital grounds will perpetuate balance, vitality, and harmony throughout the entirety of the virtual creation as long as they are visited and the rites are performed—a testament to the everlasting connection between humanity and the boundless realms. A testament to existing on all planes. Makuyeika: somos de aquí y somos de allá. We exist in all spaces and we hold it all together.

THANK YOU WITCHES.

Roma Futurism: Resilience, Witchcraft, and Technology

BY JEZMINA VON THIELE

The stereotype of the "magical Gypsy" has been a tool of oppression and survival for centuries, with Romani women especially typecast as witches. The witch in Romani culture is a complicated figure, feared and revered, known by many terms in the Romani language, including *choxani, bosorka,* and *Drabarni.*

A Drabarni is a type of healer, and uses ancestral knowledge of plants and divination to treat others' ailments or tell their futures, whereas choxani and bosorka are words to describe more fearful and powerful witches that some consider the imaginings of folk stories. Others consider them real. Words have power to them, and the word "Gypsy" evokes a sexy, mystical, even criminal archetype that has been perpetuated and appropriated for nearly as long as the Romani people have existed. "Gypsy" is often used as a slur that refers to the Romani people, and as such should not be appropriated or used by non-Romani people. Romani people are free to reclaim the word and use it however they like.

Roma are a diasporic ethnic group who originated in the region of Northern India and parts of Pakistan. A theory among linguists and historians, such as Dr. Ian Hancock, is that early Roma were likely low caste Indians circa the 10th century CE who were rounded up as an army to fight the invasions by Sultan Mahmud Ghaznavi, ruler of the Ghaznavid Empire, a Muslim empire of Turkic Mamluk origin. The invasions raged on for over a century, and in that time, the army raised families and created communities camped outside the battlefields. When the Indian soldiers were defeated, they were captured and moved west with their families into the Byzantine Empire between 1000 and 1030 CE. By that time, an entire culture of people had formed and moved west, by choice or by force. Since then Roma have been persecuted, hunted, deported, and enslaved for 500 years in Romania, targeted in the Holocaust, and continuously misrepresented. Despite ongoing persecution, Romani culture is resilient, and is preserved in our traditions, art, music, food, language, and through our digital and written records.

Ever since the Roma arrived in Europe, around the 1300s and 1400s, they were met with hostility, so few professions were accessible to them. Some worked trades like metalsmithing, animal training, basket weaving, agriculture, and performance. Other Roma became fortune tellers, using divinatory tools available as technology to develop this art of intuition, logic, and emotional support. Popular paintings by Regnier (1600s) and Caravaggio (1594) depicted Roma as both thieves and fortune tellers, untrustworthy, seductive, and dangerously other, creating enduring visual stereotypes.

Roma were likely the first people to practice divination using the tarot cards created in Italy. The cards were originally made as a game and inspired by earlier iterations of playing cards across Africa, West Asia, and East Asia. Romani people popularized and spread other forms of traditional divination such as tea and coffee reading and palmistry throughout Europe. Romani fortune tellers and witches used their skills, tools, and technologies to feed their families throughout the most desperate times. Their work was so influential that in Victorian England, society ladies had fortune telling parties and dressed up as Romani women to feel exotic and embody the aura of the Romani fortune teller. Today, non-Romani fortune tellers don Esmeralda costumes and tack "Gypsy" in front of their names to capitalize on the survival trade of the Roma, whether they realize how harmful this is or not. The marginalization of Roma is not over; Roma continue to face employment, education, housing, and healthcare discrimination. However, we are persistent and find new ways to thrive despite this.

Within Romani communities, fortune telling, or *dukkering*, or being a drabarni, is seen as a job, and can sometimes be the work of a witch too. Witches (generally speaking) are born and not made. Not all fortune tellers are witches, and some might be offended to be called a witch. Sasha Ravitch, Romani astrologer and occultist, notes that in traditional Romani communities, witches tend to be born into lineages, and there are certain signs through birth and childhood that indicate that the child is a witch. My grandmother noted that I was born with my eyes open, I went into trances, that my little toddler hands would heat up and take her arthritis pain, among other signs. I grew up assimilated and in mixed heritages, but with these signals she trained me as a fortune teller. In some Romani communities with strong beliefs in born witches of the choxani variety (though there are many other words), those witches are separated from other Roma.

While witches serve an important function as diviners, healers, magic workers, and death workers in Romani communities, they are often seen as unclean due to their abilities and their proximity to sickness and death. Witches, often born into female bodies, are not the ones who make these sexist social rules. Witch's work is marginalized and misunderstood, albeit essential. While not seen as unclean, the same can be said for a fortune teller's work, which Dr. Ethel Brooks, Romani professor of Women's Studies at Rutgers University, points out in her interview on Romanistan podcast. She explains that fortune teller's work is often denigrated because it is largely (not exclusively) women's work, and is primarily emotional labor. That labor is essential to hold a community together, yet can be taken for granted. Outsiders of Romani culture tend to see all Roma, women especially, as mystical witches or diviners, but their understanding of the concept is far from the cultural reality and laden with stereotypes.

Roma often find themselves navigating polarities—tradition and modernism, the Romani world and the gadje (non-Romani) world, the pure and the impure, the spiritual and the physical, the past and present. Romani culture today has so much diversity of experience that many Roma dismiss the idea of witchcraft as an old-fashioned superstition, whereas others live it. Our culture is ever-evolving, and Roma are adaptive, so some of these polarities coexist. Feminism and LGBTQIA+ rights still have a long way to go in the Romani community. Roma, like many persecuted groups, have internalized a patriarchal system, colorism, and other forms of oppression from the outside. However, Romani women and LGBTQIA+ folks are responsible for some of the most influential activist work within the community. The symbol of the witch, access to technology and education, and chosen family or clan (*vitsa*) have become a beacon of hope for some, and a way to embrace the beauty and power of Romani culture.

Romanian Roma Mihaela Drăgan, actress, musician, writer, filmmaker, and co-founder of Giuvlipen (the Romani word for "feminism"), pioneered the Roma Futurism movement, inspired by AfroFuturism and SinoFuturism before it. In Roma Futurism, Drăgan takes on the Romani witch stereotype and creates the cyberwitcharchetype, harkening back to the societal role that some Roma play as witches, combined with elements of sci-fi and technology. In 2014, she founded the feminist Romani theatre troupe, Giuvlipen, with Zita Moldovan, a Romani actress, television presenter, journalist, and fashion designer. Perhaps Giuvlipen's most iconic Roma Futurist play they've created is *ROMACEN: The Age of the Witch*, about Romani cyberwitches who curse fascist politicians with magic and malware, warp reality, and travel back in time to try stop the often-forgotten genocide of Roma and Sinti in WWII. The archetype of the cyberwitch is so important because it both subverts the gadje perspective of "Gypsy witches" and empowers the traditional witch of Romani culture. The cyberwitch is a savvy, smart activist who can change not only the future, but also heal the past.

Drăgan's first Roma Futurist short film in collaboration with Giuvlipen, *The Future is a Safe Place Hidden in My Braids*, is about traditional Romani witches of a family lineage: Mihaela Mincă, Casanndra Buzea, Ana Buzea, Anda Ion, and Bianca Buzea. The film is in three parts: *Enchantment for historical trauma, The Anger that will heal me,* and *The Seed of the Witch.* Drăgan does not identify as a witch herself, but as a performer who works with witches and uses the archetype as a means of empowerment. In that same vein, Drăgan writes that she is "interested in inventing a new ritual language that has the power to heal and empower Roma communities, so she updates the myths and old enchantments of Roma witches and combines them with the poetry of a modern anti-racist discourse, putting at the center of the narrative the figure of the Techno-Witch as leader of an utopian future in which the historical cycle of oppression against the Roma finally reaches an apocalyptic end." There is also a practical, magical component of the artwork rooted in what

Drăgan calls a comparison of "the ritual dimension of artistic performance with the daily rituals performed by witches at work for their clients" and she hopes that by collaborating with traditional witches, the witches will in turn heal their Romani clients with this conjoining of art and magic. The film is overwhelmingly hopeful for a future not just of equality for Roma, but also happiness. The witches, who are among the marginalized of the marginalized within the community, are the key to that liberated joy.

The vision of the joyful and powerful cyberwitch is not so far from reality. Romani fortune tellers and witches, especially the Mincă family, are finding more success in business by utilizing technology; from using Zoom to meet with clients all over the world, using reels on social media to show their services and build a following, and even televising rituals or turning them into art pieces.

In the powerful memoir, *Who Am I in the World?* Romani author and activist Rowena Marin reflects on how Roma have historically been nomadic because of persecution, and many from her community still need to relocate frequently because of the scarcity of work. Marin herself, who is not a witch but is from a family of silversmiths, left her community in order to pursue an education, as many Romani girls in more traditional communities finish at middle school and prepare to get married in their teens and start a family. Marin now works for Google, and is a big proponent of education access and opportunities for Romani girls and women especially. Access to technology and education helped Marin find the independence, stability, and abundance she yearned for. Access to technology has also created an opportunity for a different kind of digital nomadism among Romani witches, an ability to stay in one place if they wish, and expand their client base, reputation, and services beyond what was possible before, but still rooted in the old ways. Romani fortune tellers not born into a lineage of traditional witches are finding the same flexibility and freedom.

Through my podcast, *Romanistan,* alongside my co-host Paulina Stevens (also featured in the podcast series *Foretold* by the *Los Angeles Times*), we have had the pleasure of interviewing Roma of many backgrounds and professions, including traditional and modern witches, fortune tellers by trade and by discovery. Even the name, Romanistan, refers to anywhere that Roma are, and as such includes those we speak with in the digital landscape. Alice Psychic, aka The Psychic Next Door, is from a family of fortune tellers, and while her personal practice is deeply rooted in the very old ways, she has cultivated a large social media following and offers intensive online programs to facilitate healing work with clients all over the world. Kiki Robinson, aka the Opulent Witch, is an artist, dancer, witch, and fortune teller who creates digital spells that they share on social media as art pieces that followers can save as electronic sigils. They offer virtual altar tending on Patreon, and create beautiful reels that also function as digital spells. Ylvadroma Marzanna Radziszewski, aka Bimbo Yaga, artist, witch, and fortune teller, created a virtual witch school and uses Patreon to build community, especially for trans, nonbinary, and queer folks, often collaborating with Opulent Witch with endeavors like The Living Altar, which released a beautiful oracle deck made in ritual. Aurora Luna, aka Baby Recklesss, also intertwines digital art and spellwork, Patreon, and ritual to practice Western and Jyotish astrology alongside tarot and multimedia art and writing. I offer spells and conduct readings in person and over Zoom, tend ritual and teach on Patreon, and create multimedia writing and performance as magical practice. There is still discrimination, intergenerational trauma, poverty, and illness to navigate, but technology is empowering Romani witches to live a more expansive life.

The queer, trans, and nonbinary Romani witch space online is particularly alight with resources like *The Digital Altar* electronic grimoire that Ylvadroma Marzanna Radziszewski, Kiki Robinson, Aurora Luna, and I all co-edited and curated, as well as *Water Always Wanders,* an embodiment of remembered futures; a ritual of storytelling from queer Romani artists curated by Tsarina Hellfire, Ylvadroma Marzanna Radziszewski, and Konstantin Polyakov as part of Fringe Festival, a program of the 2023 Tennessee Williams & New Orleans Literary Festival. The need to create an LGBTQIA+ Romani vitsa is essential for our survival and sense of community, and is only possible if we utilize our virtual environment as well as our in-person connections.

While there is still so much work to do for Romani equality, it is not only heartening to see traditional witches cursing fascist politicians on live stream, it is life-giving. Visibility is essential for human rights, and our magic is multi-dimensional, metaphorical and literal, earthly and digital. We can listen to the feminist Romani trap witch band, Tehno-Vrăjitoarele (Techno Witches) with Kali (Mihaela Drăgan) and Niko G (Nicoleta Ghiţă), and watch their music videos of Romani witches in ritual around spaceships, and know that there really is a futurist movement happening, one that we are a part of, and the magic of it is as complex, diverse, and multifaceted as the Roma themselves.

Reclaiming Resourcing: Money Magic in This Time of Capitalism

BY JESSIE SUSANNAH KARNATZ AKA THE MONEY WITCH

If you consider prayer a form of magic—and I do—then money magic must date back as early as money's existence. Imagine our ancestors crying out in faith for their needs to be met, for their dreams to be actualized, for that debt to be forgiven. Endlessly creative iterations of money magic have existed as time has unfolded, evolving while money has taken on different meanings culturally. Modernity brought with it a spectrum of both atrocities and advances in resource distribution. Money magic, like many magics, is personal, and impacted by personal circumstance—a wish whispered or shouted at an opportune time, a plea for comfort and ease handed over to the cosmic powers that be—as unique as a person's financial circumstances and baggage.

Most modern money magic focuses on one of the following areas of individual experience: road opening (calling in new opportunities), prosperity (a longterm and sustainable state of wealth), abundance (a state of more-than-enoughness), fast cash (magnetizing money to attend to an immediate need), good luck (as with gambling or lottery), career luck (new job, a raise, success for our business), or getting out of debt. Historically, communities did their resource magic (such as rainmaking) together, co-creating with the environment and the immaterial realm through an animist lens. This may have taken place through sacrifice, tithing, temple practices, veneration, and prayer through dance and song.

As large-scale gratitude and offering practices were shut down via colonial religious consolidation, short harvest festival "holidays" hung on as the vestiges of these strategic magical systems. With an anti-Indigenous worldview embedded in our minds and our schedules, most of us have forgotten the daily and seasonal practices of offerings and sacrifice, merely stopping by to say thanks once a year. The tenacity of these festivals through so many centuries shows how central resource magic and ritual has always been. What has been protected through syncretism is the most precious and the most essential of what our ancestors wanted to pass on to us.

In capitalism, getting our material needs met shifted from a communal endeavor supported by collective ritual, to an individual and nuclear family quest, and our money magic reflects that. It is hugely disappointing to many of us to live in a time where survival means money within racial capitalism. It is my personal spiritual belief that our souls meet our particular body and a particular point in geography and timeline on purpose. Which is to say, your particular "Earth journey"—your human incarnation and the circumstances of it—is intentional. If you are here, now, it means you are essential to this moment and this moment is essential to your soul's growth. This is the classroom that your soul has been assigned to and this is the curriculum. We are each weaving a thread of human evolution that is on a trajectory toward healing. So if you are here in the midst of late stage predatory global racial capitalism, this economic ecosystem is a part of your assignment.

As part of an instinct to divest from the hellscape of modern economics, lots of us view money magic as selfish and capitalist. This instinct is paradoxically influenced by the internalization of puritanical Christian ideologies on wealth. As empowering as it might be to believe our individual efforts could be that impactful, resisting money, disavowing money magic, and avoiding one's personal finances does absolutely nothing to destroy capitalism. Money itself is not the same as political economic power, nor are trade and the marketplace. The instinct to view money magic as capitalist is strengthened by the ways in which many modern money magics, such as the Law of Attraction, have rooted in the white supremacist tendency to spiritually bypass blatant realities of systemic inequality and its impact on financial, mental, emotional, and physical health, all of which have "money" consequences.

We have a great invitation to uncollapse these ideas—money, money magic, and racial capitalism—with the goal of getting to the root of what money magic and a deep relationship with the entity of money have to offer us—the opportunity to stand fully in our power and sovereignty to create worlds. We are invited to practice a radical modern money magic, rooted in communalism and respect, and to remember money magic as a counter magic to the spell of capitalism. We can reorient our money magics in service of financial healing—individual, lineage, and collective—and find it gives us a deeper capacity to be powerful contributors to liberation culture.

As with any liberation work, our first job is to let go of perfectionism, and simultaneously remember that, as Kenneth Jones and Tema Okun articulated, perfectionism is itself a characteristic of white supremacy culture. Perfectionism and "purity" are not liberatory because they are not humane. In our activism and in our healing, we have to stay working on the edge of what brilliant witch Sanyu Estelle Nagenda calls "the relationship between urgency and infinity." Seeking a purely anti-capitalist money magic while being steeped in the system is more of a hypothetical exercise than a sustainable practice for most people.

Practicing money magic right now means doing money magic within capitalism, because doing money right now means doing money within capitalism, and that's okay. Our role is to stop being afraid of money and money magic, learn about its power, and then get innovative. Playing with and exploring possibilities for anti-capitalist money magic is a visioning and a dreaming forward toward the future we want to be a part of. This can look like large scale magic momentum against systemic forces—such as Inés Ixerida and Lacey Johnson's Hex the Patriarchy invocation. Much of this magic will be personal, carried out in our day to day practices—in our kitchens, yards, front porches, and pockets, as well as in our bank accounts and businesses.

The high priests of "the economy" want us to be afraid of money because it lessens our political power. It is essential to remember that capitalism is itself a magic spell. The practitioners of capitalism and colonialism have never doubted their power to influence the course of events, nor have they shied away from invoking their Gods as a source of their power. This invocation of supernatural forces is intentional yet subtle because it is normalized as religion.

Even more esoteric traditions, such as the Masons, are seen as normal white men just meeting about their business. These magicians have captivated a majority of the global population and left even those of us who actively resist with a sense of confusion (internalized oppression) as to how natural and long-standing capitalism will be. They excel at concealing their manipulations in order to protect against counter magic, using normalization and glamor magic to distract and impress us. The spell is cast through the mythologies of colonialism and capitalism—bootstrapping, willpower ethic, survival of the fittest, poverty as a moral failing, nationalism, eugenicist body standards masquerading as public health information (for example, Body Mass Index). As magicians ourselves, we know how powerful words are, and as cultural workers we know the power of storytelling. The first tactic of capitalist magicians is to use shame (again, internalized oppression), concealment, and miseducation to keep us financially disempowered.

It's impossible to talk about money without talking about power, just as it's impossible to talk about magic without talking about power. My working definition of magic is taking responsibility for yourself as an energetic entity. When you acknowledge your impact you step into both personal power and communal responsibility. In acknowledging ourselves this way, we are invited to acknowledge the personal power and responsibility of all beings. This calls us to get intentional with how we direct our energy as well as how we fulfill our responsibilities to the Earth collective.

Magic work draws heavily on alliance. When we set our intention through ritual, spellwork, altar work, and other forms of craft we often ask other energetic beings (such as stones, plants, birds, elements, archetypes, Spirits, ancestors) to align their energy with us in the direction of our intention, sharing their personal power with us. In the second tactic of capitalism as a magic spell, we see a perversion of the concept of magic—instead of an invitation for other energetic bodies to ally their energy toward an intention, we see an exploitation, a coerced harvesting of energy to direct toward a cause. This aligns with the capitalist worldview of all resources, including human lifeforce, as an available resource to align with their intention—creating and consolidating capital.

The third tactic of capitalist magicians is to leverage religious power to consolidate state political power and wealth. Religion is an enclosure, a statehood built in the immaterial world. At its best, it is a powerful facilitator of relationship between humans and the divine—a creative and ecstatic reflection of culture. At its worst, it's a tool of social control used to cement emotional allegiance to state ideology. Many times it's used as both. In a hegemonic religious framework, certain dealings with the supernatural are sanctioned and others are not. Witchcraft, Paganism, and brujería, among other terms, have been used as political dumping grounds for state-unsanctioned relationships with Spirit, including whichever Indigenous practices a given colonizer was trying to economically undermine at the time. This tactic is designed to consolidate power through instilling fear of marginalized spiritual practices, categorizing what is deviant and what is holy. It can be enacted as genocide, "holy" war, and more subtly as emotional and intellectual disdain for magical practices and thinking.

These beliefs run hundreds and even thousands of years deep in some ancestral lineages, with the Christian Roman state's response to what was seen as a religious threat established in 186 BC through the mass persecution and murder of members of the Bacchic cult. Keeping people afraid to practice or of being accused of practicing anything that might resemble a marginalized spiritual practice hinders most people from utilizing their magical personal power, which economically benefits empire. In day to day life, many of us make almost no distinction between folk magical practices and religious practices, joining our ancestors in the subversion-within-assimilation practice of mixing and matching from the menu whether in public or private. The distinction is not personal, it is political. The difference between magic and a miracle is what the official religion of the state says it is.

A radical modern money magic will incorporate counter magic against capitalism into our individual pursuits for success. By remembering others in our money magic we can reclaim collective resource spells. Recognizing the necessity of including all members of our communities in our prosperity work is healing work. Magic as a witch requires relationship building with the Earth and Earth's inhabitants, unseen spirits, and extraordinarily ordinary people. We deserve to be resourced, and the desire to be so does not make us evil or capitalist. Our ancestors knew that resourcing the collective was a necessity, and doing so in right relationship and through negotiation with the spirit realm creates the conditions to peacefully receive. Capitalism teaches us to pursue one sided relationships that bring us resources, magic teaches us that building in mutuality and collectivity will cultivate complex and holistic wealth. This relationship building also extends to our relationship with ourselves. We do our financial shadow work to be prepared for participation in the world we want to be a part of. Healing our money wounds is the work of preparing with intention to show up to the collective. This is money magic as well.

It is so understandable to be discouraged at this time in our collective journey, and yet we must accept our collective healing processes as nonlinear, just as we accept our own individual processes to be so. Our human story is the perfect illustration of the fact that healing is not linear. We are part of deep time, of everything that is, was, and ever will be. Our job is not to save humanity from capitalism. Our job is to show up with presence in our relationships, and that includes our relationship to money. You only have two jobs in this incarnation—be you and stay alive. Staying alive means material survival and being you means doing it as the genius, creative, subversive, integral and magical person that you are. Money magic holds a rich herstory of helping people access personal power and community resourcing from the margins, and you are a part of this story if you choose to be.

CHAPTER 3

DECOLONIZING WITCHCRAFT

Reclaiming the Power of Lineage,
Mythology, and Sovereignty

Throughout human history witches, healers, medicine people, and spirit workers have been oppressed, demonized, and colonized by dominant groups attempting to usurp and assert their power. Traditional indigenous practices of working with deity, communing with the land, and healing through touch, plant, and sound, have all been repressed or wiped out systematically by colonial movements across the planet. Christianity alone has been a powerful force in co-opting Pagan beliefs to encourage colonial domination of peoples everywhere. The time of the European Witch Hunts represents a period when religious and capitalist forces systemically squelched any and all sources of community care, personal sovereignty, and sovereignty over the land, in order to control all manner of production and labor. By dismantling indigenous and traditional methods of communing with the sacred power of the land, and the power within ourselves, colonizers oppress and exploit all of us. This insidious colonial project is still alive and well today.

Despite all of this trauma and real danger, witches have persisted to exist and practice. The knowledge of indigenous wisdom ways, the practices that have healed our ancestors and their intimate connection with the spirit world, have been preserved despite the threat of danger and ruin. These practices and wisdom ways persist precisely because this knowledge is sacred, necessary, and our human birthright. As modern witches, we exist within a capitalistic and materialist culture that strips cultural context and spiritual meaning from anything it can; this capitalist white-washing is a dark spell which keeps us from honoring our roots, knowing our histories, and prohibits us from celebrating our differences. Witches stand in active defiance to this dark spell, through reclaiming our lineage traditions, magical technologies, and the myths of our ancestors, while respecting the cultural wisdom of other cultures through nonappropriative engagement. Decolonizing your witchcraft involves a reclamation of blood lineage, cultural lineage, and indigeneity.

One of the greatest psychic illnesses born out of this colonial project is an epidemic of loneliness. We can attribute this loneliness to many things, but without a sense of belonging to a community, without a sense of home found in the land we occupy, and without a sense of relationship with our ancestors, we flounder, seeking meaning and purpose in cultures outside of our own. The following offerings are stories, dreams, and ritual to support you in regaining a sense of belonging. May these witches inspire you to continue the deep and often challenging work of reconnecting with ancestral allies, communing with your magical lineages (they exist, if not buried and hidden deep in the Earth), and honoring the cultural legacies that you hold.

—Casey

Tracing the Thread of Belonging Spell + Ritual

BY KIKI ROBINSON AKA OPULENT WITCH

I reimagine the idea of belonging
As I find home within my being
My altar seeks self-commitment
As I make vows to my magic
I belong to myself

Through the support of the elements as ancestors, we can invoke time magic and our spirit of creativity to explore the sense of belonging and trace it to the root of connection. This spell and ritual involves dissolving false glamours and illusions of belonging, exploring the wisdom of our earthly form, and traveling with curiosity.

The intention of this exploratory ritual is to create openings in relationship, conversation and dialogue with aspects of "Ancestor" that feel distant, cut-off, and inaccessible. This is one approach to remediating and reclaiming autonomy, belonging, and connection and counter-acting symptoms of isolation and Imposter Syndrome that stem from systemic oppression. This ritual is intended as a "hello," and a relationship tender. As witches, we hold our magic and wisdom in the altars of our body, and can work with the elements as ancestors to create accessibility and remember our roots of indigeneity within our magical practice. This ritual is intended to awaken your altar to this process in a way that invokes curiosity and creativity.

As a collective ecosystem we are traversing what we call as the "Tower Times"—evoking the archetype of the Tower of Destruction in the tarot which symbolizes a deep dismantling, release, and reckoning within the current

62

A CONFLUENCE OF WITCHES

structures of the systems which we are living in. What comes after The Tower, is none other but The Star—visions! Renewed hope! Dreaming and inspiration! We can only connect to the Vision of the Star and collective wellness if we begin and continue to cultivate belonging and reconnect with our roots.

How do we define belonging within our craft and altars as witches? How do we reconcile with the historical relationship of disconnection cultivated by systems of kyriarchy? How can we reclaim belonging and shatter the spell of isolation? *How can we open the door to a space of connection and belonging within our altars and magic?*

Belonging is a sense of safety, security, and acceptance. Everyone deserves belonging. It is essential to our basic needs to feel held and embraced by a community, to be witnessed, and to feel a sense of connection. We can consider belonging as a homecoming to a deep root of connection. In the magical realms we might experience this as a coming home to a primordial or ancient space, an origin point.

When we feel our basic needs are being met, we are more connected to our own magic, to supporting others, and receiving care. Feeling a sense of belonging can also engender a sense of purpose, service and understanding our role(s) within greater community.

When we feel a sense of belonging within our craft and practices, we feel connected and in honorable relationship to our altars and spirits, we are rooted into integrity. When we are uprooted from our values and searching for belonging, we often act out of character or grasp onto anything to feel a sense of connection, even when it is outside of our sphere or wheelhouse.

HOW CAN WE RE-DEFINE CONNECTION AND COMMUNITY?

Intimacy is interdependence. I am one spark in the rich fire at the hearth of mutual care. My roots are nourished in the ecosystem of collective well-being. I set my gaze upon the liberation of all, knowing that when we are all free to bloom so too is the true power of relationship.

—RELATIONSHIP SPELL FROM *THE LIVING ALTAR*
BY KIKI ROBINSON AND YLVA MARA RADZISZEWSKI

Connection and community is a resource and relationship. We are in relationship at all times—with ourselves, our spirits, the spirits around us such as land and place, nature spirits, plant and flower allies, fungi ancestors, cosmic and celestial allies, planetary beings, familiars and animal kin, our human friends, chosen family, acquaintances, and partners. One way we can access those connections, when not immediately accessible, is to turn toward our spirit allies, bright + well ancestors, plantcestors, queer + trans ancestors, and guides. It is crucial for us to reclaim the roots of belonging in order to heal, before we move into visioning, dreaming for the future, and creative expression. When our basic needs around safety, security, and stability are met, we can begin to access creative solutions, imagination and self-exploration.

WHAT GETS IN THE WAY OF BELONGING?

We can consider the systems of oppression—white settler colonialism, capitalism, and cis-het patriarchy—as collective curses which hold sentience and express themselves through thought-forms, belief systems, behaviors, and cords. Oppressive systems hold both external and internal impact. We often internalize these systems and it manifests as perfectionism, shame, imposter syndrome and the role of scapegoat and outsider, only to name a few. These collective curses may cause us to feel like an outsider looking in.

Byproducts of these systems are false glamours, illusions, and delusions that create a sense of urgency to belong, so we grasp at belonging wherever we can find it, often outside of our own root system. This felt urgency makes us susceptible to "trying on" another culture's practices without tending a relationship with that lineage, or spiritually bypassing in order to fill the void.

BEFORE WE DIVE INTO RITUAL: FOUNDATIONS AND PREPARATIONS!

Before beginning the ritual, we must prepare, cast a circle, shield, and set up our space! Preparation for ritual work is essential to creating a supportive process. Boundaries are essential to exploring magical realms, protecting ourselves, and creating parameters for our work. Psychic boundaries and self-clearing techniques are important to our practice because it allows us to be energetically safer, discerning, and clear in our workings and our daily life. Know your energetic fields intricately. Cultivate tools and techniques to claim and maintain sovereignty.

WHAT IS TIME MAGIC?

Time magic is working intentionally with Time as a medium to expand, contract, slow down, speed up, and travel. Time magic dissolves the binary, and is inherently dismantling of structures that seek to oppress because these structures thrive off of linear time. Time is a resource; having time sometimes means having spaciousness, ease, and relief. Let's remember that the constructs of Time by capitalist standards are inherently ableist, *and* we can trust we have the power to work with the fabric of time in a way that benefits our healing and magic. You might already do some form of time magic already and not even know it. If we can identify time magic as intentionally (or unintentionally) dissolving binaries, it is safe to say that being a queer, trans, and/or nonbinary human comes with the gift of time magic!

On Creating Sacred Space

First it is important to cast a circle. Casting a circle is a way to declare that it is a space of sovereignty and protection and also clears distraction and nonsupportive energy. Cast a circle in the way that is most integrally aligned for you. . .

PROTECTION

Psychic Protections can be visualizations, physical ritual and spell work, and invocations that create buffer, glamour, and boundary for our energetic, spiritual, and psychic body. If you already have a relationship with shielding in your practice, you can use your own method. I love working with mirrors. Visualize layers of mirrors surrounding you, and ask that these mirrors be invoked with fire or element of choice, to shield you from anything that would not support your work. Or imagine a ring of cobalt blue fire around you: imagine it burning away any psychic attack, any harmful energies, and anything that is not in alignment with sovereignty.

OFFERINGS

We make offerings to the spirits we work with to create a reciprocal and right relationship, which allows them to receive the life force of the offerings and be nourished and fed as we raise energy for ritual. When we open the portal to the ancestral realms often there will be hungry spirits that are in need of sustenance.

Offerings can include but are not limited to: biodegradable offerings such as flowers, fruit, coffee, water, tea, liquor, juice, food, sweets, and herbs. Offerings can also be: prayer, song, poems, dance, music, art made as an offering, fire such as candles, smoke, cigarettes/cigars, and incense. If you know what your ancestors have enjoyed, make offerings of favorite food and drink.

. . . .

Tracing the Thread of Belonging Spell + Ritual

You will need:

- About three feet of red thread or string

- Scissors

- Cinnamon stick

- Candle

- Broken watch or representation of time (if you do not have access to a broken watch or other representation of time, you can use an image)

- The root of an ancestral plant ally (if you do not know ancestral information, make an offering and prayer for a root to present to you on a walk or at the store)

- Paper + art supplies of your choice

- A comfortable, quiet place to create sacred space

1. Prepare your space and gather your ingredients. Begin by creating your altar. This can be unique to you. Make sure you have representations of the elemental spirits because we will be working with them intimately. Place your items to charge on the altar, make offerings to the spirits and ancestors.

2. Cast a circle to create a container of sovereignty and protection. Call to your bright + benevolent ancestors, allies, protector spirits, and your Spirits of Creativity. Invoke Time Magic; ask Time to soften, expand, and dissolve.

3. Honor the spirits of land and place where you are residing. When we facilitate magic, we are borrowing from the environment around us. We do not want to create further disruption or harm, so it is important to ask consent and raise energy for the spirits of land, especially if you are on stolen land due to colonization. Learn the histories and original stewards of the land, give reparations, and move forward humbly and in reverence.

4. Begin grounding with Mother Earth, allowing the Earth to bring up supportive energy that can resource your heart and nervous system. You can take a few deep breaths here to slow.

5. Take some time to do some self-clearing; clear distraction, psychic debris, filters, false illusions, glamours, and distortion. Take this time to really hone your internal sight and intuition. Notice where there is fog or haze and envision a Fire transforming and cleansing this energy.

6. You can now connect with the Spirits of Creativity, which is a facet of you, yourself as muse, the inner Visionary, glimmering with inspiration. With your art materials, mediate and call forth a symbol or sigil that holds the energy of connecting to your roots, dissolving false narratives and illusions, and connects you more deeply to the magic of your lineages. Draw, paint, make marks, be open to how it comes forward onto the paper. Place it on the altar when you are finished.

7. Next, take the red thread and tie the broken watch or symbol of time to one end and tie the root to the other end. This represents the thread traveling back to the root of connection. Place the symbol of time in one hand and the root in the other. Act intuitively.

8. Make yourself comfortable and begin to breathe. Invoke a trance-like state as you invite the elemental ancestor of Air to connect in, allowing the hand with the root to gently be guided to your lungs and breathe, tracing it over your body. Call to the Ancestral Spirits of the winds and sky, remain curious. Greet and welcome Air as Ancestor.

9. Next, invite the ancestor of Fire to arrive, tracing the root and thread to an area of your body that symbolizes fire—this might be your heart! Invite every fire that your ancestors held to be present in this moment, say hello and connect to the Ancestral fires. Notice what you sense.

10. Begin to call to the ancestor of Water, tracing the root to an area of your body that symbolizes water, maybe this is your tears, be open and allow this to be an exploration. Call to the Ancestral Spirits of the bodies of water at the root of connection for you, say hello and connect to these energies. Notice what you sense in your body.

11. Begin to call to the ancestor of Earth, tracing the thread and root to an Earth area of your body, this might be your feet. Call to the Spirits of earth, land, trees, plants, fungi, and flowers that are ancestral for you. Be open to what you notice, hear, sense, feel, and see. Say hello.

12. Now that these Spirits have arrived in council, this can be a time of conversation, connection, and healing. Allow this to be exploratory and curious—maybe you want to move your body, maybe you are craving stillness, maybe you want to write. Be in this space as long as it feels supportive.

13. Lastly, tie the red thread to the stick of cinnamon along with the root and symbol of time. This symbolizes the opening to lines of communication

and healing. You will place this on your altar and allow it to work for the next lunar cycle or as long as it feels right.

14. When you are finished, you can give gratitude to the spirits and elements as ancestors. Begin to call yourself back home into present time as best as possible, as you begin to close all portals that were opened. Compassionately disinvite the spirits and beings that arrived, and reinvite back those that were disinvited. Close your container and wrap up your work.

15. You can keep the altar up for a designated length of time or dismantle it and give your offerings to the Earth. Allow there to be integration and remain open to new insights and openings around more rooted connection.

· ·

There Is Sustenance in the Roots

BY STAR FELIZ

Morning glory vines grow in a winding pattern. I imagine that when they sleep at night their energy goes down to the roots to replenish their medicine and receive sustenance for the next sun.

Medicine is beyond the plant materials and its applications. Medicine is a complex yet simple system. (You will read many ideas that seem like contradictions throughout this text, as it's my queer shapeshifting trickster way of illuminating.) Root medicine gets to the "heart" of the issue. Root medicine is the saline water that covers most of our earth. Root medicine is grandparent medicine. Root medicine is a dance between the dead and the living, the seen and unseen.

Truly knowing myself in this world of extractive capitalist colonial racist patriarchal paradigms has been a real life mythic journey. There's the flowers of my individual expressions, there's the leaves of my accumulated life experiences, the stalk of my purpose that connects me to the world, and there is sustenance for body and spirit in the roots. Root work is necessary work. Root work is freedom work. Doing my root work allows me to live with integrity, know where I come from, and stay true to my bones even in times that call for me to rebuild the whole house.

About the most important thing I've learned is this: that the mysteries are alive within us. Go deep within your own mystery which is a gateway to the mystery of the cosmos. So I hope my story lands on your path like empowering medicine.

Loving Connection Is the Salve

*black sails fly the ship breathing out fire in the cooling coos of the
river. one uglied storied bird, neck coral, is chewing images to digest into
words. sense cents count too many unnamed.*

In my dream, I was being shown a blue black sea. From the perspective of
an atlas, the waves were made of electricity and a storm was always in the
weather forecast. There were souls moving as one body and swimming in the
sea in the shape of a large human cargo ship. It felt like an eternity. Later I
would dream I was viewing a scene unfold as the sun was at its highest point.
Out of the corner of my eye I see someone who feels like a queer ancestor. He
stops to wink at me with dainty white and yellow flowers tucked behind his
ear and then rushes on down the bushy hill toward a river. He freed himself. I
turn my head and a group of white men in blue militia uniforms. One of them
was heartbroken.

The influences along my medicine path are many. I'm a child of hybrid
ancestry with a Gemini moon living in diaspora and raised in an eclectic city
with friends from all over the world in the 21st century—so it's only natural.
My influences include Tibetan and Thai forest Buddhism, Christian mysticism, Ayurvedic healing, Mayan cosmology and healing, and reiki to name
the most constant. But the riches of ancestral medicine traditions were always
there in my home and in my life. They were just waiting for me to wake up
and see them and claim them, in my own way, in the way I only know I can.

Dominican Vodu or *21 Divisiones* is a religious-spiritual tradition that's
practiced in community with other humans, spirits, and the natural world. It's
a spiritual way of life that grew uniquely from the soil of Ayiti and its cauldron
of West African, Taino, and Southern European lineages. Devotees are called
servidores or servants of the mysteries and a *caballo* or horse for the great spirits. The biggest barrier to me fully embracing my roots was the familial silence
that accompanies generational shame and trauma. Being Black, unschooled, a
mystic healer, and living your life on the land (AKA being a *campeniso/a/x*)
meant having little to no opportunity under the ruling class paradigms. So it

often meant carrying the shame of being poor, marginalized, and denied dignity. But the plant spirits have been there from the beginning, unlocking doors to memory no matter how painful or repressed.

I still remember the first time I learned about my ancestral connection to certain pomegranates for instance. I was in the kitchen slicing up probably my second whole pomegranate that month, a fruit I adored dearly. I committed to paying $5 for it at the supermarket, even though less than $10 is often what I had. My mom watched me break open the fruit to reveal the seeds and complained about how it stains everything. "Tu sabia que a Tata siempre le encantaba la granada?" Tata, her grandmother, had always loved pomegranates. She went on to reveal that the ground outside their home was always red because it was covered in pomegranates and there was more than could be eaten by them all. On her lot of land, my great grandmother also grew tobacco, aloe vera, and other agricultural medicinal plants.

There was also a feeling that I never truly belonged to my culture. Yes, insert all the things about growing up a poor immigrant kid in Uptown NYC who's also visibly Black, a bookworm, queer, sensitive, and goth punk (you might've heard that story before). Yet what drove me to delve deeper into my medicine practice was a fierce love for my people, our afro-latinx/indigenous cultures, and a fierce love of this earth. I hadn't yet resonated with anyone working to connect human culture and nature together in ways that acknowledged and worked to uproot oppressive systems, but I felt it was possible. As a teen I was lucky enough to receive some glimpses at experiencing embodiment as I hiked along the Appalachian trail, and as a young adult when my permaculture mentor Marc Robbi said to me, "Nature and culture aren't separate. Remember that the root of agriculture is culture. This work is the first culture." For years after that I would go on to learn more about myself and this human relationship to land through active decolonization work and research in archives.

I've learned that we cannot live the stories of others. We can honor the past and be inspired but we also have to trust the timely rhythm of our own ever unfolding experimental story lines. Just like we deserve expansiveness, imagination, and space, so do our ancestors! I still remember visiting the only panel about gender at a well known conference about slavery and raising my hand at the end to ask about how the enslaved may have preserved the legacy of multiple genders and sexualities in indigenous African societies. The academics snickered: "We cannot queer the past." We also must not recreate transphobic historical erasure. Now, thankfully, there are thinkers and writers working to "queer" slavery.

What is it that shuts down our imagination enough to believe that anything beyond this present reality was never possible? I've learned that separation from our source is our greatest wound and loving connection may be the only salve. So while the rest of the world is content in chasing illusions, connect with the earth below your feet for they are ready to teach you so much.

The Mysteries Are Alive

you are the rebirth vulture spirit cleaned a path for. the one who will free our bellies up from silent rage. we dreamed and fed on the spark of rebellions. tres ojos wept our bitter tonics for desires unexpressed.

In my dream I'm standing still as many are running with fear past me. The ground is rich cinnamon reddish brown. The sky feels low and the vegetation is so green. But there is chaos and brutal violence in the air. I turn around and I see the biggest tree I've ever seen in any reality. It's the essence of the world tree. And there are brown bodies hanging from its trunk. They've been tortured and left to bleed out. I see a handful of uniformed men walk slowly around the other bend and I know I have to keep moving. My grandmother finds me and we take shelter in her dark shack making sure our only candle-light remains dim. She tells me everyone in our family is gone. We fear these are our last moments together.

There is a broken medicine lineage within my family that I've been (and many of us I'm sure are) tasked with revitalizing in the world as the lineage holders. The lineage holder of Dominican Vodu and Cimarrón folk healing that was practiced by my ancestors and then buried due to fear, shame, trauma, many circumstances within and without, and not allowed to pass on.

I know this because of my many dreams with ancestors and divination sessions. The root work, the soul work. On my last trip back to visit mami, I was able to connect the dots that my mother and my grandmother were both not raised by their mothers. They both had to abandon their children in order to survive, due to physical disability, immigration, financial poverty, and flat out chronic traumatic violence. This wound is deep and there is so much pain, resentment, and feeling of not belonging that I witnessed within all of them—and myself. I was raised by my mother but on a different land, and she wasn't always emotionally and physically present.

This helped me understand so much about staying for love and having to leave because of love. And it helped me put another piece in the puzzle of my maternal healing line. My mother would tell me stories of how my great grandmother would have conversations with the dead and feed the family and all the street kids with just one meal. There's more reason to shrink your power when your greatest example of that power was taken away from you.

21 Divisions is a celebratory earth and cosmic spirituality rooted in community life. My greatest sense of home has always been in my creative process. When I began to notice the voices of the elemental spirits come forward through my artwork, I channeled this energy into an experimental devotional musical project called Priestusssy. With Priestusssy, I'm carrying forward the trance ceremonial dance and musical aspects of Dominican Vodu that heals viewer and _caballo_ alike, and weaving together my knowledge of various folk medicine practices. Song has allowed me to trust my own compass through the spirit world, because it's going to feel different for all of us. For example, when great spirit is getting ready to lift me into another dimension, it's through feeling like I'm floating below water that I know it's time to travel and be shown new information.

It's always worthwhile to take the time to know who you are and why you are here. Understanding my way of traveling and accessing various realms, like a felt sense of this being shown to me as a past life, or an ancestral vision, or etc, is empowering. It's liberating to have awareness over your own sign system and overall path. With deep trust in ourselves our magic is undeniable and needs no external validation or unjust gatekeeping. I may not feel like I fit in anywhere still, but my queer mutant magic belongs and is more than needed in this world.

and So the Story Continues

*we now enter the depths of the caves **again** to pick up our power and reemerge with gold dripping from ori. oh daughter, water is born from your well.*

It had been the first day in my two week long Wilderness Medicine training on Coastal Salish land. In my waking life I was getting ready to fall asleep under a maple tree with a large artist conk fungi growing from its trunk. In my dream my grandmother was looking at me but pointing to a wall of tobacco plants in front of her. The world of tobacco was a spectrum of purple and pinks and maroons and green. Everything was vibrating like it was breathing in a cosmic psychedelic wavelength. They were in this world but they were not of this world.

My decolonial ethics and yearnings want me to go back, have an entangled relationship with the Dominican Republic and claim it as home. My queer knowing tells me that home is not a destination. That home is safety and belonging and it's within me. And it's within communities that have taken me in. A country was never that for me and I'm not sure if it was for all of my ancestors. I find belonging with the earth and among people who hear the earth's rowdy sexy call. So I make peace with being the lineage holder who consciously plants roots under a new sky.

Our medicine is mystery. The mysteries of the earth, the cosmos, ourselves, and the cycles of the evolution of consciousness. The mysteries are more commonly known as *Los Misterios.* Los Misterios of 21 Divisions comprise a cosmology of forces that have been with my family for generations. Shifting and changing as we've shifted and changed in lineage. The healing lineage of this medicine is extra-sensory. It's a personal relationship with creation. My queerness, my gender fluidity, my inbetweenness and expansiveness is a reflection of the mysteries. Everything is alive.

My gender is fluid like the lines between the spirit world and the material world are fluid for me. The special role of lesbian, gay, queer, two-spirit, and trans people of the Caribbean is represented in the Haitian *loa* Ezili Dantor and in Santa Marta la Dominadora of 21 Divisions. Along with being powerful healers and creation spirits, they're collectively the caretakers of orphans, the elderly, and sex workers. Their spirits are revolutionary and everyone knows they're not one to be fucked with. With written histories being a reflection of the colonizer's imagination—How do we hold our closeted/fluid/passing kin and trancestors that survived or thrived beyond the documents? And trust that gender and sexuality have a shitton of expressions? What do we hold on to? What do we make peace with and evolve from?

I think about the important role Ezili Dantor played in the Haitian Revolution and how we're currently living through many critical pages in history. In a conversation with my friend Quito, they illuminated for me that the wisdom of gender and sexual transitioning can aid us collectively in transitioning to just societies. Let us come home. Other worlds are possible. An old world is dying and a new world is sprouting within ourselves. How will your medicine be activated?

Preserving the Witch

BY KIMBERLY RODRIGUEZ

As a child, there were mornings when I would wake up to the house smelling of copal and coffee. The smell would force me to open my eyes and I could see the dainty lines of smoke that looked like tiny ghosts making their way into my room. The tiny ghosts would float around, twirling and dancing with one another, completely enveloping in each other's presence. It was beautiful to watch. The smell of coffee was the real reason I would get out of bed in an instant. In a Mexican household, there is no such thing as having no coffee or *pan dulce* (sweet bread) in the mornings. I knew that when amá brewed a fresh batch of coffee, that meant there was pan dulce! And when there was also the smell of copal, that meant *amá* was up to something.

Copal is used to cleanse a space, bring calmness and help with spiritual ventures. Copal is a staple in a Mexican household as it is a resin that our Mesoamerican ancestors used for sacred rituals. Coffee is a great offering to our ancestors as it helps awaken their spirit to be present with us. Copal, coffee, and sometimes pan dulce—that is how amá oftentimes chose to start her mornings and a practice that I continue today.

Preservation is the intention behind my practice. As a detribalized indigenous woman, it is vital for the survival of my lineage to preserve practices, rituals, recipes, songs and the language of my ancestors. Like many folks who have been disconnected from their roots due to the horrors that colonialism birthed, reconnection is only possible through the preservation of our roots which includes all the ways that our ancestors deemed as sacred to live as and live by. As our major society forces us to adapt to a normalized way of living that is not suitable and oftentimes harmful for some of us, especially marginalized communities, the preservation of our roots is how we can live in a safer and loving environment. When we preserve the sacredness of our roots, we are preserving the medicine that we each hold, and this is a revolutionary stand against the diaspora and genocide that has occurred within many of our communities.

The Revolution

In today's major society where many injustices continue to be prominent, where prejudices against sexual orientation, race, age, class, culture, and persons with disabilities continue to exist, a revolution is necessary. A revolution would not be necessary if our major society would care for the well-being of every*body*. A revolution is never an act of spite but a stand based on necessity. We need a revolution to get to a place where preservation is possible.

Revolutions today don't necessarily mean we gear up and physically fight. Revolutions today are based on how we choose to live in opposition to harmful regulations that do not suit our wellbeing. How we choose to live today speaks volumes about how our future will look, not just for ourselves, but for future generations of our lineages. Revolutions today can look like adapting certain practices that take into consideration our mental health, our physical health, and our spiritual wellness. They can look like choosing to incorporate ten minutes every day to sit down and relax our nervous system by breathing deeply and attentively rather than just starting the day head on without preparing for the workload ahead. It can look like choosing to teach your siblings, children, family, or friends recipes that are significant to your culture so that the recipe continues its legacy within loving community. Revolutions today are not armed with firearms or weapons, rather they are waged through our conscious decisions of choosing how to live instead of being told to live in corrupt/capitalist ways.

The Witch

For as long as I can remember, I have been drawn to the archetype of the Witch, and though I didn't realize it then, it mirrored something to me that I would later find out lived within me. That "something" I would eventually find embedded in my roots, in the passed-down rituals and recipes from my *abuelas* (grandmothers) and mother, in the prayers and *remedios* (remedies) that I grew up hearing and seeing others perform, in the shuffling of cards that abuela Toña would carry with her everywhere she went. Nobody in my family called themselves a Witch, rather they labeled themselves as healers, or acknowledged their gift as just a *presentimiento* (feeling)—a deep knowing of what to do or say in certain instances. But in essence a Witch is just that—they are healers, they are intuitive forces that can be in service to others, but most importantly they practice in service to themselves, to preserve and continue the legacy of their lineages and ancestors.

The mornings when my home smelled of copal and coffee as a child, I knew amá was calling upon her spirit guides. She often talked to them in prayer, in silence, or by drifting into a long and deep stare. Amá taught me the importance of the unknown, of speaking and praying to the unseen, as they are the guides that help us in our earthly realm. Copal and coffee in the mornings were her signature invitation to call upon her spiritual guides and, soon after, it became my own signature practice.

I am a witch and I fully embrace this title. My magic has always been profound, but it became ignited when I intentionally and consciously decided to walk the path of my ancestors. It is part of my practice to preserve the simplest of rituals such as the one I adopted from amá. Offerings of copal have long been a Mesoamerican practice to be given to our spiritual guides and ancestors. When I carry on the rituals of my ancestors, I know that I am being protected and loved. I feel a sense of belonging and gratitude. And in a society where we are told these feelings should be overlooked or that they are unimportant, our revolution starts here—by fully embedding ourselves in the human and spiritual nature of what it is to feel safe, loved, to belong, and feel gratitude for finding this space of comfort.

The Journey

Preservation is how we move forward as Witches, as healers, teachers, guides, friends, neighbors and individuals. There is nothing without the preservation of the sacred. Our ancestors have always known that through preservation we continue to breathe life into the spirit of our lineages. And though some of our ancestors may have done more damage than good, we can always choose to restore and start a new pathway to healing by being in right relationship to the earth, with our neighbors, with our bodies, and by practicing sacred reciprocity in all encounters, especially where we are constantly learning or consuming from Black Indigenous People of Color. As some of us seek to regain bits and pieces of an erased history from our ancestry, remember that we all come from somewhere, we all have established roots no matter how little or how much we know of them. May we reconnect in any way that may be accessible to us and trust that we are being guided and protected by forces that have our greatest intent in mind. Preservation and reconnection can start with a simple Google search or having conversations among relatives that may know stories of our ancestors.

This journey is not a short one nor a comfortable one. Truths may be uncovered that are hard to bear, friendships may be lost, unsettledness may take over, and you may sit and wonder if you are doing the right thing. I often find that during moments of uncertainty when "trusting the process" is not enough to ease my nerves, I close my eyes, take a deep breath, and let the air move its way from my nose to my chest. I take a moment to let the air settle in my chest and after a few seconds of containing the air in my chest, I not only realize but I also feel how strong and capable I am to do what feels right in my bones, in my blood, in my body. Preservation is my journey and I welcome you to also be a part of this journey. As I tend back to my copal and coffee mornings, I offer you the following prayer to start your preservation journey, Tlazohcamati;

On days of dim and rays I vow to uphold a legacy that calls upon my bones.

On days of a weathered down terrain

I remember I am as strong as stones.

On days when I question my creation

I commit to love and glory.

On days when I forget my path

I stand in gratitude and this is how I ignite my preservation.

CHAPTER 4

WE GATHER IN SPIRIT WORLDS

Betwixt and Between Allies, Guides,
and Supernatural Wisdom

A SACRED THREAD THAT WEAVES through the work of most witches is a resonant understanding of Spirit as a connecting principle. Some folks call it Goddess, some practitioners call it the sacred, others understand spirit to be magic
itself. No matter how one works with or defines spirit, it is understood to be a
ubiquitous shaper of reality, an invisible glue that holds all of creation in relationship. Beyond that, spirit is multifaceted and multidimensional, showing
up as deity, energy, archetype, ancestor, and elemental ally. No matter how you
practice, witches each have a very personal relationship with the divine, and
their own methodologies of communicating with it.

As witches, guided by spirit, we navigate the world with a heightened sen-
sitivity, ever aware of the subtle currents through which spirit flows. Whether
we are attuning to the emotional baggage of our coworkers or being haunted
by lost souls in our rental flat, we experience the world as a multidimensional
field of matter and spirit. For witches, the unseen world of spirit is just as
real and important as the world of TikTok and redwood groves. Traditionally, a central aspect of witchcraft in many cultures and lineages is to work
consciously and collaboratively with a host of spirit allies. These spirit allies
range from ancestral spirits, to otherworldly entities, to spirits of the land, to
guardian angels. Modern witches are constantly navigating a complex web of
spiritual contracts, between those spirits who we consciously choose to work
with and those who call upon us to commune with them. Spirit contact is a
dynamic and reciprocal art—one that comes with surprising blessings and
very real challenges.

Largely, the work of communing with spirit is an affirmation of the sentience of our cosmos. When we are young, we are often more aware of the
spiritual matrix of our experience, before we are conditioned to believe otherwise. The energy of trees, the spirits who dwell in our homes, the energetic
makeup of our families are all more accessible to us before materialist or religious conditioning takes hold. Witches resist societal conditioning that disbe-
lieves in the spirits of home and hearth, denies our direct participation with
the divine, or those who have trouble acknowledging their dreams as spirit

communications. As witches, we are both attuned to the animism of the universe, and constantly shaping our embodied relationships with a host of spirit allies. There is always a choice in how you relate to the cosmic kin.

Consider how you define spirit in your own life. How does the divine communicate with you? How are you in communion with the divine? May your understanding of spirit expand through learning new ways to receive spirit messages, connect with new ancestral helpers, and through questioning the fabric of spirit itself.

—Casey

Creating a Spirit Guide Language

Strengthening Your Connection to the Unseen Realm

BY AJA DAASHUUR

Embarking on the path of developing our intuitive and psychic abilities is a profound and transformative journey, and one that every being has access to. However, along this path, we often encounter self-doubt, an inner struggle that challenges our ability to accept, receive, and activate the medicine offered by our Spirit Guides. This battle with self-confidence can hinder our progress, leading us to sand down the messages and insights we receive, ultimately diluting their power and impact. It is crucial to recognize and address these doubts, allowing ourselves to fully embrace and trust the wisdom of our spiritual gifts.

Self-doubt can stem from various sources, including societal conditioning, comparison to others, and fear of judgment. To overcome this, we must nurture self-belief and cultivate a deep sense of worthiness. Comparing yourself to others only serves to undermine your confidence. Embrace your individual spiritual journey and honor the guidance that flows through you by recognizing and affirming that your intuitive and psychic abilities are unique to you.

Self-doubt in a spiritual practice can lead to hesitancy and reluctance to act upon the guidance we receive. To break free from this pattern, we must embrace courageous action. Trust that the messages and insights from your Spirit Guides are meant to guide you forward on your path. Step out of your comfort zone, take inspired action, and witness the positive impact it brings.

Remember, the more you align your actions with the guidance received, the more your confidence in your abilities will grow.

At times, self-doubt arises as a result of questioning the authenticity of the messages we receive. We may doubt whether the insights truly come from our Spirit Guides or are merely products of our imagination. It is important to acknowledge that our imagination and intuition work hand in hand. Our subconscious mind and Spirit Guides communicate through symbols, imagery, and intuitive impressions. By accepting this dynamic interplay, we can open ourselves up to receiving profound wisdom and guidance.

Through my own experiences and deep connection with the unseen, I have developed a powerful tool called the Spirit Guide language key. This key serves as a pathway to connect with those who reside beyond the veil, unlocking the possibilities of communication that were once hidden. As a dedicated Spirit Guidecoach who has immersed myself in the study of the spirit realm for several years, my passion lies in helping my community expand their awareness of their unique spiritual teams and cultivate meaningful conversations with them.

In the realms of spirituality, the concept of Spirit Guides has long been cherished by those seeking guidance, wisdom, and support from the other side. By developing a unique language that resonates with our spiritual team, we can experience signs, symbols, and intuitive impressions that expand our understanding and strengthen our relationship with the unseen realm.

Our spiritual teams can include ancestors, angels, souls we have lived with in past and future lives, even animals. It's really quite extraordinary the various types of Spirit energy that we have surrounding us at any given time.

When I guide individuals on their spiritual journeys, a personal language key evolves and grows alongside their connection to their guides. This key becomes a living, vibrant tool that enables them to navigate and explore the depths of their spiritual relationships.

Working with and creating one's own Spirit Guide language key in community is akin to embarking on a shared quest through the realms of the unseen. It's like having a special, ethereal language that binds us all together as we seek higher understanding and deeper connections. As we converse with our Guides, we not only gain profound insights into our personal paths but also uncover universal truths that enrich our collective consciousness. It's a bit like learning a new language; as we become more fluent in this spiritual dialect, we find ourselves more attuned to the subtle energies around us. As we exchange experiences, interpret signs and symbols, and share messages from our guides with others, our collective understanding deepens. It's a beautiful tapestry of diverse experiences woven together into a shared narrative of spiritual awakening. Our Guides become trusted companions on our journey, offering guidance, solace, and inspiration.

The Language of the Soul

A Spirit Guide language is not limited to words or symbols; it is a sacred expression of our soul. It taps into the depths of our being, allowing us to communicate on a profound level. This language can manifest as sounds, symbols, visual imagery, or intuitive impressions that are deeply personal to each individual.

Signs and Symbols

Our Spirit Guides often communicate with us through signs and symbols, acting as messengers from the other side. These signs and symbols are unique to each person and hold personal meaning. As we develop our Spirit Guide language, we become more attuned to the signs and symbols presented to us. For example, my guides began by showing me a path—a metaphorical journey. Sometimes the path was clear, accompanied by blue skies, while other times an individual would appear to the side of the path or seem stuck in a certain mode. This imagery provides me with valuable information about myself or the person I am connecting with, forming a core part of our language. It allows me to ask questions based on this imagery, helping me gain deeper insights and understanding.

Creating a Spirit Guide language requires us to expand our perception of reality. It necessitates acknowledging that our imagination and subconscious mind play significant roles in receiving information that our conscious mind may have ignored due to societal programming, doubt, or fear. By embracing our innate psychic abilities and accepting that our imagination works hand in hand with our spiritual abilities, we enable our subconscious to receive information that our conscious mind may have filtered out. This expanded perception allows us to access a wealth of knowledge and insights that strengthen our connection to the unseen realm.

Trusting Our Intuition

Developing a key also involves trusting our intuition—the inner knowing that transcends logical reasoning. Our intuition serves as a bridge between the conscious and subconscious realms, enabling us to tap into spiritual knowledge and receive guidance from our spiritual team. As we cultivate trust in our intuition, we become more attuned to the subtle messages and intuitive nudges that guide us on our spiritual path. Through trust, we deepen our connection to the other side and develop a profound level of communication with our Spirit Guides.

Developing this trust is a deeply personal and creative process. It invites us to explore and embrace our unique ways of expression, allowing our inner creativity to flow freely. Whether it be through writing, art, music, or other forms of creative outlets, we have the opportunity to express our connection with the unseen realm, and thereby honor and affirm our intuitive impulses. Through self-expression, we open up new avenues for communication and deepen our relationship with our spiritual team. Embracing our authentic self-expression in connection with our Spirit Guides strengthens those bonds and enriches our spiritual growth.

Creating a Spirit Guide language is a transformative journey that empowers us to strengthen our connection to the unseen realm. Honing a Spirit language involves acknowledging and interpreting the signs and symbols our spiritual team presents to us. By expanding our perception, trusting our intuition, and embracing self-expression, we develop a profound language that resonates with our spiritual team and our conscious mind. Through this language, we deepen our understanding, receive guidance, and nurture a profound relationship with the other side. Embrace the power of your Spirit Guide language, and witness the expansion of your spiritual journey with clarity, purpose, and divine support.

Intuitive Exercise: Building Your Spirit Guide Language Key

Find a quiet and comfortable space where you can focus without distractions. Take a few deep breaths to center yourself and relax.

Connect with Your Guides:

Close your eyes and set the intention to connect with your Spirit Guides. Visualize a golden light surrounding you, creating a protective and loving space. Invite your guides to join you on this journey of developing a Spirit Guide language.

Ask for a Symbol:

Ask your guides to show you a symbol that represents their presence or a specific message they have for you. Be open to receiving whatever comes to your mind's eye, or any other sensory experience. Trust your intuition and allow the symbol to unfold naturally, whether it is visual, auditory, or even a physical sensation.

Observe the Symbol:

Once you receive a symbol, hold it in your awareness. Take a few moments to observe its characteristics. Notice its shape, color, texture, sound, or any other sensory details that stand out. Pay attention to how it makes you feel and any intuitive impressions that arise.

Seek Meaning and Connection:

Reflect on the symbol and its potential meaning. What does it represent to you? How does it relate to your spiritual journey or the guidance you seek?

Trust your instincts and allow your intuition to guide you in making connections between the symbol and your spiritual team.

Engage in Dialogue:

Begin a silent conversation with your Spirit Guides. Ask them questions related to the symbol and its significance. Listen for any intuitive insights, impressions, or words that come to your mind, or any other sensory experiences that provide guidance. Be patient and receptive, allowing the communication to flow naturally.

Record Your Experience:

After the dialogue, take a moment to write down your experiences, insights, and any messages received. Keep a journal dedicated to your Spirit Guide language journey, noting the symbols, meanings, and any ongoing conversations with your guides. This will serve as your personal language key.

Practice and Expand:

Continue to practice this exercise regularly. Explore different symbols, ask for specific guidance, and expand your Spirit Guide language key. Be open to receiving symbols through various senses, whether visual, auditory, or sensory. Over time, you will develop a unique and personalized system of communication with your spiritual team.

Remember, developing a Spirit Guide language is a process that unfolds over time. Trust your intuition, stay open to the signs and symbols you receive through different senses, and allow your connection with your guides to deepen. With practice and dedication, your Spirit Guide language will expand, providing you with profound

There's Something about Mary

BY AURORA LUNA AKA BABY RECKLESS

Most modern societies are conditioned by Christianity in some way. Living in the US and/or living with religious trauma can make connecting with anything related to Christianity hard and uncomfortable. That's the funny thing about the craft; you craft too close to the sun and next thing you know, the work gets hard and uncomfortable. Shadow work and transmutation are integral to a witchcraft practice and have to be attended to for any healing and resilience to grow. Often, during the deeper witch work, unexpected allies make themselves known. It's at these crossroads in our craft where we get to decide whether we spiral over the desired forms of help not given, or accept and utilize the help that was not only needed but actually arrived. . . When many people find themselves going deeper into their practice, they hit ancestor work and quickly find that it's no longer "their way or the highway" but a two way street. Often at this crossroads we meet Mother Mary.

This piece isn't to convince you of why you need to work with and accept the help of Mary—that's each and every person's own journey. What I can tell you is that if your ancestors are bringing Mary to you, she's much more than what you are probably imagining. She opens the door as more than just Jesus's mother, even though that is an important part of her story.

Mary connects us to the Goddesses and spirits of the past. If you look into her history, you'll see just how intertwined they are with ancient Goddesses. Often her sanctuaries were built over old Pagan sites of worship, so it stands to reason why there are so many apparitions that show up and speak to whatever culture she finds herself in. She exists as so much more than what any church presents her as, and this is evident in the various folk practices found around the world that incorporate Mary into their cultural practices and rely on the church in name only, not in praxis. There's a mystery about Mary. When she shows up for you, she presents you with the keys to open the door to those secrets.

If you are at the point where you want to begin that journey, here are six simple ways to connect with Mother Mary within your already established spiritual practice:

1. Start adding Mary to your prayers in the morning and at night. You can come up with ones on your own or use prayers from the Christian canon. I personally like to use a mix of both, as I truly believe in the power of words and repeated prayers continuing to bless and protect throughout time and with continued repetition. Canon prayers most of the time have intended purposes and, as Mary has been a major pillar of Christianity for ages, there are a lot of prayers to choose from.

2. Add Mary to your ancestor altar. If you are already immersed in your ancestral practice and lineage and need an apparition of Mary to start with, research what Mary your ancestors would have appealed to. You can also do divination to connect with your ancestors to ask about their Mary practice (see divination prompts below), or ask Mary herself. When asking Mary to send signs, don't be surprised if a medal or prayer card shows up in your life quickly!

3. Many people see Mary as the "spirit" of their house in addition to their ancestors and any other deities and spirits they may work with. Incorporate prayers and workings with Mary when you do any magic concerning your home and hearth. Pray to her while cooking your favorite meal. Pray over and consecrate her images for protection around your house.

4. Light a novena candle for her during the new and full moons. Start each lunation with a practice that affirms your intentions and pray for nine days into the next cycle you are about to experience, grounding yourself and surrounding yourself with love and support on your journey. Dress your candle with corresponding herbs and oils that align with your intentions. Your new moon candle is for new intentions that grow as the moon

grows, and the full moon candle is for releasing and removing as the moon becomes smaller.

5. Connect with the rosary and the mysteries it contains to connect with Mary and your personal experience of her. If you are new to this practice, I recommend practicing the traditional rosary and mysteries. Pay attention to the story it tells while focusing on Mary and her actions and the journey she takes. Put yourself in Mary's shoes: how would you react to the things she experienced? Can you see the strength and power she exhibited in her life? Can you see why and how your ancestors worked with her in their lives? Are you inspired by this? Are there any new areas you can see asking Mary for help with, or be inspired by her story to take aligned action? After you gain a personal understanding of the prayers and mysteries as shared from your own gnosis and the gnosis gained from Mary and your ancestors, you can begin to incorporate your own prayers if you feel called. You can create rosaries for specific intentions and rituals and use these prayers as spells within themselves. The rosary becomes not just a meditation tool but a portal to your ancestors and the Divine Mother as well as a magical tool.

6. Mary is often compared to the High Priestess card in the Tarot and is known to help in matters of all kinds of divination from cartomancy to dream work. If you feel called, dedicate a tarot or playing card deck to Mary and place it in a container with herbs such as rose, mugwort, and lily, along with a prayer card. Pray over it for thirty days while connecting with her each day. This is a simple way to deeply connect with Mary's power of prophecy and knowing. She can also help you to understand and receive messages from your ancestors and other spirits as well.

This is a divination spread to connect with your ancestors about who Mary was to them and who she can be to you:

1. A card to represent the Apparition of Mary in your life right now as brought to you by your ancestral lineage.

2. How she showed up for your ancestors.

3. Why your ancestors are bringing this to your attention now.

4. How can you connect with this apparition of Mary.

5. A message from this apparition.

These are just a few suggestions to get you started. Trust your intuition, be open to Mary and the messages she sends, and receive the ancestral mysteries being revealed to you.

Loving What Is: Quantum Witchcraft

BY SANYU ESTELLE

Engaging with the "the Quantum Realms" (as I know them) means accepting that there are multiple dimensions and multiple realities. Infinite ones, in fact. All truths are true at once, just from different perspectives. All truths being true doesn't mean all truths are relevant to your truths, or that every truth is meant to be a relatable truth, or even that every truth that is relevant for you is a "Universal Truth."

The Quantum Realms engage with you regardless of whether you are aware of them or intentionally engage back. The way(s) you choose to respond are always your choice. In the Quantum Realms "Universal Truth" can be defined as Multiversal Truths because Existence is infinite. Where "Existence" represents all that is and will ever be, including everyone and everything we have ever known or will know.

This reveals the shape of what Quantum Witchcraft is, a practice that honors multiversal truths.

What if *loving what is* and allowing all that is (that you are aware of) makes you more of yourself, and is actually the quickest route to your most preferred self and world? Where "preferred" is defined as the versions of you that you would most love to be in every circumstance——both those circumstances that you determine and those that you do not determine.

Then the only thing keeping me from my most preferred self is me. What do I embody? How do I choose to embody it? These things are up to me. I do not get to determine all the circumstances of what happens to the many versions of me that I am over the course of my life, because I did not create all these circumstances. I didn't even create myself. But I choose myself by continuing to be myself and by taking the reins of what I allow myself to become.

This doesn't mean I haven't been influenced by others and things outside of me. I am not an island. An island isn't even an island. Only I know what parts I choose to believe of what I am told, what I experience, and what I perceive. . . I am doing my thinking for me and as me. I define the world as I know it.

People can say they are in there (you) with you, they can even indoctrinate you or force you into circumstances that you don't prefer; but they can't keep you from learning what you choose to learn from your experiences. They can't keep you from having the character that you most prefer to have, regardless of your circumstances with them or others. And they can't keep you from becoming the best person that you are capable of becoming.

The etymology of Power means "powerful; lord." The definition of Power ranges from, "ability to do or act; capability of doing or accomplishing something," to "the possession of control or command over people; authority; influence." For a word that means itself, Power = Powerful, we impose many meanings on it. It is curious that we assign Power the meaning of will and we assign power the meaning of force. These things aren't synonymous to the people who have had to learn the difference.

Witches are the kind of people who learn the difference between will and force. The kind of power that people have sought to have over others is only the power that they *think* they can have or that they think they have (influence, authority). It is not power (simply being powerful) itself. Power as a concept is something that humanity noticed while being of and in nature. Power is not something people created. It is not something people determine. To learn that and how "the ability to do and act" is not synonymous with "the possession of control or command over people" takes experience and knowhow.

Our relationship with Existence supersedes our relationships with each other, and any power dynamics we can have between us and other. Because without Existence we would not have self or other. Not even the invention of humanity—no matter how much it fights to do so—can keep me from experiencing, witnessing and learning from all that Existence is to me, for me, with me and of me. I am the only one who is within myself, so I am the only one who can decide (*for me*) from within myself what is outside myself.

The etymology of Identity literally means "the same" or "as it, as that one." It is a concept that suggests continuity through relationship or recognition. Identity is simultaneously an observation of what is within and what is without as well as an observation of how we relate to ourselves in contrast to how we are related to others. Without an identity there is no craft to witch about. To identify with oneself as any particular self is to construct the foundation of belief upon whatever witchcraft proves relevant to that self.

As a self-identifying Quantum Witch, the "I" of me that I am and choose to identify with (and/or as) at any given time is limitless. I am made unlimited by the fact that I can change. At any moment I can choose differently than I ever have previously. In doing so, I can create a ripple effect that shifts the dynamics of an entire ecosystem that was formerly "my world," "my country," "my community," "my family," "my reality," etc. At any moment I can change my character completely and redirect my history.

Concepts that define belief systems that are more monolithic, binary, triadic, or limited aren't defined in the same way from the quantum perspective. Things always change. This is how we remain limitless/infinite/eternal, remember? So change is canon in Quantum Witchcraft. I don't view the known or the unknown as hostile or as in conflict with each other. I don't maneuver as if Existence or anything within it is working against me.

This doesn't mean that from other's perspectives they aren't working against me. This doesn't mean that on a systemic level things haven't been constructed to limit how or who I am or become. It just means that for me to believe you can work against me is also to believe that some aspect of Existence can work against me on an existential level. I don't believe that Existence works against or contradicts itself. So, by extension, neither myself nor others can work against or contradict me *fundamentally*. Everything simply has degrees of differences.

Existence goes by many names: God, Life, the Universe, the Multiverse, All That Is, The Powers That Be, Great Spirit, The One, Gaia, and so on. I stated, "our relationship with Existence supersedes our relationships with each other" because we each have a direct line to Existence, which makes possible everything within it including whatever we're in seeming opposition against. I don't have to be beholden to humanity's relationships with me to determine my experience of life itself. Nobody does. At the end of any given day, it is the individual that decides and defines what Existence, God, the Universe or the Powers That Be are and mean to them.

In spiritual and esoteric work, or in witchcraft, there is often a hyper focus or overemphasis on "changing things" as if change must be tempted and isn't always already happening in the greater framework of reality. Too often we are presented with the craft or "the work" (ancestral, spells, shadow, etc.) as something we should utilize to "fix" our circumstances. There can be a uniformity in approaching our experiences as if they are wrong and it is our individual and/or collective job to "correct" these experiences until things are right (according to us).

However, if you view Existence as being in proper order, "What Is" as being in alignment and Earth as being perfect, what then is there to change or to fix? It is one thing to share your perspective, it is another thing to enforce it. If you are the one that perceives things as out of alignment, it is you that you need to assess, or change or relocate. You are the only person you're living from. Your perspective is the only one that you have full designation and autonomy over.

Because of our nihilistic, patriarchal, classist and globalized social conditioning, we have learned to view control and power as if they are synonymous with force, abuse and oppression. We often dismiss the negative mechanism of employing force when it is on a systemic level because we become conditioned into thinking it is the natural order of Existence itself. But just because humanity does something doesn't mean it is necessitated by Existence. There is nothing outside of us forcing us to *believe or do* anything.

We have conditioned each other to believe that choice is limited and intellectual. That it's determined solely by the faculty of the mind, that our intellect is "superior" to our other senses, faculties or intelligences. We consistently see examples within humanity of people attempting to overpower the will of body, the will of emotions and even the will of nature by depending upon the will of their minds. Rather than explore these connections with regard or appreciation for them we resent them and use our energy to work *against* them.

We have been conditioned to view emotions as less informative than the intellect and we have been conditioned to view the body as more grotesque than the mind. Yet it is our emotional intelligence that determines our choices. Even when we identify our choices as intellectual, the intellect is attempting to recreate a state of being or a place of feeling that was experienced *emotionally*. Joy, desire, pleasure, pride, satisfaction, contentment, peace, euphoria, passion, ecstasy, fear, defensiveness, appreciation, anger, betrayal, jealousy, disdain, self-righteousness, embarrassment, shame? These are emotional states of being.

No matter how much we try to intellectualize our way out of feeling, emotions are intrinsically human. To be human is to feel things. Just like to be human is to have a body. But even the body has been sublimated in favor of the intellect. Fatigue, overstimulation, disease and disability are all pushed aside in favor of our ideas of what "should" be happening. Our body isn't allowed to be sleepy or uncomfortable because we demand that it complies with our and other people's intellectual ideas. We are taught to ignore our physical states of being.

For our intellectual intelligence to be satisfied with our bodily intelligence and our emotional intelligence, we would actually have to appreciate what those other intelligences are and how they show up for us personally and collectively. Within Quantum Witchcraft, emotions are recognized as legitimate forms of intelligence that we embody so that they can be utilized; and the body is validated as an intelligent organism that is predisposed to assist with our world perspective, our life's journey and the nature of our witchcraft.

Quantum Witchcraft celebrates all forms of intelligence, validating the natural harmony that can exist between the intellect, the body and emotions. The craft is a tool of celebration and appreciation. It doesn't exist for us to constantly be on the defensive, plotting or planning for what we think we know will happen. A big part of divesting from the doctrines of nihilism, patriarchy and classism is appreciating What Is. What Is (which is Existence's responsibility), what is for you (which is your primary responsibility) and what you are willing to do about whatever there is that you can do about what is happening for you.

When we learn how to appreciate What Is within Existence, we'll also know how to appreciate everything else. The craft part of a Quantum Witch's work includes dealing with What Is by considering one's perspective, changing one's beliefs, taking more aligned actions, allowing for one's experiences, and coming to know oneself differently. If you aren't living your truth, reflecting upon your beliefs, conducting yourself differently when engaging with circumstances you don't prefer, and learning through osmosis, then by what means would you actually know yourself from a different perspective?

CHAPTER 5

WITCHCRAFT, BODY, EARTH

Look to the Rhizomes and Mycelium:
Situating Your Magic in
Your Relationship with Earth

AT ITS CORE WE FIND THAT WITCHCRAFT is a spirituality that honors the body and a working of the sacred and basic elements of our existence to affect change. Our bodies themselves are ecologies, ecologies that collaborate within organic power systems with their own capacities and limits. Dancing with this awareness brings the interconnection of all things into sharp focus. Our lives are a collaboration with countless microorganisms, stars, Earth masses, bodies of water, and other beloved kin. Witches have an intimate awareness of this interconnection, which strengthens our awareness of our own internal and bodily sources of power. Ultimately, this animistic worldview recognizes that all elements of the cosmos are sacred. Our bodies are cosmos themselves.

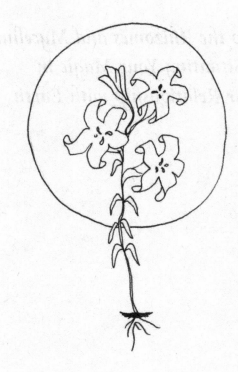

We witches participate in a dynamic and reciprocal way of relating with all of creation. Whether it be working with plant medicine to heal and awaken consciousness, or communing with nonhuman kin to expand our awareness of human's capacity to communicate, witches have ways of tapping into the deep resource of intelligence that exists in all organic forms. Animistic approaches to the world offer a richer, more potent experience of wisdom, a wisdom that is much needed as our precious planet faces climate collapse. Witches listen to the wind and gather chamomile at the Solstice because they understand the subtler forms of psychic emergence that is available to them when they are co-creating with the Earth and honoring all the cycles of their body and Earth's body.

Understanding the Earth as an extension of self also puts us into contact with the spirits that dwell in the land. The relationships we build with our other-than-human kin have the ability to heal our false sense of isolation, as well as repair so much of the harm that has been perpetrated in the name of human supremacy. As the world struggles to regulate its fragile systems, and climate catastrophe becomes more extreme, the friendships we form and nurture with the Earth will be the frontline for collective reconciliation of the atrocities humans have committed in the name of endless growth and greed. May witches everywhere begin and continue to nurture those precious friendships with the land, its many precious creatures, and the spirits who dwell in those last wild places.

—Casey

Flower Animism: A Floral Spell

BY LIZ MIGLIORELLI

Animism is the essential, emanating root of my embodiment, magic, and herbal practice. I hold the perspective that every being is possessed by its own conscious, innate wisdom, and that humans are not the only intelligence that inhabits the cosmos. My magic continually responds to the great fabric of life that I am woven into; the land is the source of this practice. The medicines I make are shaped by listening to the living song of the plants, the seasons, the animals, the waters, the stones, the ancestors, the weather and the stars. Animism is how I practice kinship with the world; I am in relationship with nonhuman entities that include spirits, gods, the elementals, landscapes, and most frequently, flowers.

Both medicine and magic flow through the flowers. One of my most beloved ways to work magically with the green-blooded ones is by crafting flower essences. Flower essences are vibrational catalysts. They are vessels of transformation. While essences are seemingly subtle, they are also incredibly profound, bringing the waters of our own bodies into resonance with the floral realm. One of my herbal teachers, Atava Garcia Swieciki, says that flower essences are nature's tuning forks. When we work with an essence, our energetic bodies calibrate to the frequency of a particular flower. The vibration of this flower becomes a part of our composition, a part of our song. I feel the flower as a current, as a spur, as an undulating distillation.

An essence is prepared when a flower is in fullest bloom; when they are exclaiming to the world, *Here I Am! In My Most Radiant Expression!* It is *this* unique, most-potent pulse of the flower that is imprinted into a bowl of water and preserved with some kind of alcohol, traditionally brandy. Flower essences do not contain the physical constituents of flowers that we often rely upon in plant medicine; instead they are naturally vibrational. In Western herbalism, flower essences are used to transform our consciousness patterns, to shift our emotional experience, and to stimulate spiritual opening. In magical practice, a flower essence is a spell.

If one definition of magic, according to Dion Fortune, is *the art of changing consciousness at will*, to take a flower essence is a manner of spellcasting: to change form, to shape shift, to become other. Essences are a form of magical practice, each essence is a distillation of a flower's will. Witches know that any change in the web reverberates and affects the whole. Small changes, even the most ethereal of vibrations, can be amplified with intention. To take an essence is to become very precise with our intention, to move into deeper presence and connection with something outside of ourselves.

To Conjure A Place

The Wild Iris is a beacon. On the Mendocino headlands, the scattered flowers form a deep purple blanket that shimmers as the wind moves through the tall grasses above the Pacific. Year after year, I made my way to the cliff edge to be with them in late spring when they were in bloom. I brought my essence-making bowl, spring water, tiny bottles, and notebook. The ground of this particular Iris patch is a place that I visited almost daily, all throughout the year; I have napped, cried, watched the sea birds, danced, picked up trash, prayed, feasted, stared at the ocean for hours, and sat with the flowers here. This particular spot was a most treasured place for me, there at the edge, wild with wind and whale sightings and the gloaming purple of the iris flower through the heavy fog. My spirit is woven into this cliffside. Over the years, I have made a total of four flower essences from this particular patch of Iris; and now that I am planted across the country from this beloved Iris ground, when I put a drop of this flower essence on my tongue, the Mendocino headlands return to me, the crashing tides swirl in my veins. I can feel the great expanse of the ocean in front of me again, the saltwater mist in the air and the visionary beacon of the iris flower. The magic and medicine of this place dwells in this small bottle between my two hands.

To deepen this animistic floral framework, flower essences can also be a way to listen to the great conversation of the land. Essence crafting is a form of place-based storytelling; they are stories of distinct ecologies. Not only do the essences hold the pattern of a certain flower, they also contain the expression of the land where this essence has been made. We cannot separate the plant from the sparkling web of life that gives the plant spirit, vitality and form. The Linden tree outside my window is in relationship with the angle of the sun, the pollinators, the soil, the wind, the mycelial web, the stream near its roots, etc. I also believe that Linden expresses the ancestral memory of the land, the land spirits and the myths that have sprouted from this very bedrock. All of these vibrant elements are a layered story that a particular essence may hold. An essence of yarrow that has been crafted from a plant that I have cultivated in my garden in New York is going to have a completely different energetic flavor than a wild yarrow plant that is growing in the high Sierra mountains. These place-based remedies infuse the particular medicine of an ecology into our bodies.

Active Kinship

Making a flower essence is a ritual that honors the relationship between the essence maker and the plant. Whether or not you consider yourself a plant person, it is likely that you have had a meaningful experience with a flower that has altered you in some way. There was something about it—the beauty of the flower itself struck a chord, the color of the petals, the shape, the way the light made the flower glow, the scent, *that feeling of touching on a deep mystery*. It is almost unspeakable. To see that flower, that plant, and feel it ring like a bell from within you. The flower that opens up worlds for you. The flower that enlivens your energetic and psychic senses. The flower that in just meeting alone offered resonant wisdom, felt like a poem, told you the oldest of stories. You remembered something secret and holy in this meeting. Enchantment moves between you. You are changed by it.

When this kind of inspired meeting happens, when a plant touches you in this deeply embodied place, we recognize it as a big moment. Because of our Western cultural disposition toward extraction, it is common to experience the urge to possess the magic of this plant that we have been offered a glimpse of, to harvest the riches of this meeting for ourselves. We feel so moved by the power of it, that we try to claim that encounter as ours, as something we can own and put in our pocket. However, our attempt at possession or pursuit dulls the experience of kinship. We try to claim it, to clutch at it, but the nature of this encounter is ephemeral, just like the spring ephemeral flowers.

An essence is not extractive, nor does it try to possess. My practice with essence making is rooted in an act of devotion, honoring that moment of transformation when we meet a plant that is a key to our inner world. We do not have to harvest any parts of the plant to get in touch with its medicine. For me, making an essence becomes a ritual practice that honors that moment in which I can feel into resonance with a certain plant; it anchors me *here*. Essence making is a ritual practice that honors the ways in which the story of this plant shimmers through the world. Essence making is a practice of recognition, of being called into presence to all of the Earth's magic.

There are many flower essence teachers who believe that it is wrong to imprint your own energy on the plant while making an essence. When I first learned about essence making in herb school, I tried to remove myself as much as possible from the practice. I was told that my energy did not belong in the process and that the essence would be ruined if I even touched the flower with my own two hands. I was taught that if any part of *me* was involved, the essence wouldn't be pure. This concept of creating "pure" essences still is very prevalent in the flower essence world.

Now, I reject purity with essence making. I want to break the illusion of our own estrangement from nature. This is part of the magic of essence making, we remember that we are not separate.

I follow instructions from the plants themselves. This instruction is received after a long period of observation, listening, and asking permission. For me, making an essence becomes a ritual practice that honors that moment in which I can feel into resonance with a certain plant, it anchors me in the here and now. At this moment in my practice, essence making is less about the final product and more about what happens during the ritual of making it. What happens when we turn toward the flower. I bring my offerings, my prayers, songs and poems to the flowers. I have used the essence ritual space as a way to invoke ancestors, to pray, to shed, to rage, to dance and move energy, to write, to draw, to cry, to cast a spell. . . I try to allow whatever surfaces a place in this process. The act of crafting an essence is many things: a celebration, a coming together, a meeting, a collaboration, a dance, an invitation and a conversation. It is a practice of tending, of responding to the world.

An Animist Framework of Rooted Practices for Essence-Making

Before making the essence:

- **Make daily observations about what you notice outside your home.**
  Begin with where you are, today. Head outside first, instead of to the books, to see what emerges. Let us begin by grounding, bringing presence to where we inhabit. Where do you sit in the web of this ecology? Where do you sit in relation to the ancestors of this place? What elemental layers of spirit live here—earth, fire, water, air—and how have they shaped the land you are on? What animal familiars are here? Can you learn the indigenous names of the place where you live? What are the mythologies of this place? How does weather express itself seasonally? Are there certain streams, street corners or trees that speak to you? Spend time here, bring your offerings, sing your songs, and begin. There's no rush to derive meaning or extract medicine from these observations at this time. This practice can take days, weeks, years, many lifetimes. But the more we sense and feel into the multidimensional fabric of life around us, the richer our medicine making and relationship building will be.

- **Draw a map of the land around you.** What land spirits are present? I live next to the Muhheakantuck River. This river informs so much of my experience of life here, on Munsee-Esopus-Lenape lands. I can't see the river from my house, but I know it is nearby, a large part of what it means to be a part of this ecology. Using a piece of paper, draw out the shape of land around you and what feels resonant and powerful to you. This is not a map of precision, naming or definition, but of feeling into the bioregion of where you are. This can absolutely include human-made structures—are there places that hold significant energy to you?

- **Bring devotional offerings.** Before I make an essence, I spend time (sometimes years) building a relationship with a certain plant. I visit this plant, pray to them, and leave offerings. An offering is a bridge between the human and nonhuman realms. What are your offerings? Even better, share your intentions with the plants and ask the plant what you might offer. Listen deeply for a response. Make sure your offerings are biodegradable. The more you spend time here and leave these offerings, the stronger the bond becomes. The desire for building relationships feeds the devotion.

- **Ask permission.** I always ask a plant if I have permission to make an essence. I want this ritual practice to be consensual. If I receive a *no*, I honor the *no*. It is absolutely okay to receive a *no*. I can ask again at another time. Sometimes a plant says *no* for years before I receive a *yes*. If I receive a *no,* this doesn't mean that the relationship ends. If anything, it is an opportunity to show up more fully. There are some plants that are still saying *no*. Many plants say *yes*.

Making an essence:

- You will need: a glass bowl, water, a 1 oz. tincture bottle, offerings, at least 80-proof alcohol to use as a preservative, a nontoxic flower that you have received a yes from, and your notebook.

- Prepare yourself. How do you ground and bring yourself into awareness for essence making? The idea isn't to "purify" yourself, but to feel into intention and connection. Sometimes I burn herbs, other times I bathe myself, sometimes I fast.

- Go to the flower. Say hello. Make your offerings. Ground and call yourself into presence. Pour the water into the glass bowl and place the flower in the bowl. (You do not need to pick the flower, you can also lean the flower over the bowl, or place the bowl at the base of the plant.) Let the flower infuse into the water. While this is happening, notice what arises for you. What do you notice happening around you, what animals do you hear around you, what is the wind like, what is the astrology of the day, what are you thinking about? Take notes. Read a poem to the flower. Better yet, write a poem to this flower. Dance while the flower dances in the bowl. Sing a song. Give thanks.

- Bottle the essence. When you feel that the essence is done, strain this essence water into the 1 oz tincture bottle. Only fill the bottle halfway with water. You really just need a little! Fill the other half of the bottle with alcohol.

- Take a sip from the remaining water in the essence bowl. Feel the magic. Write down what you notice. Offer the rest of the essence water back to the Earth. Give thanks.

Telling the Bees: Communicating and Relating to the More-Than-Human World

BY ARIELLA DALY

Our senses are not our own. They are shared with something far greater than our individual experience. Yet, it is our delicate sensory perception that keeps us vibrantly relational to the the world around us. We know that how we communicate between humans is far more textured than language alone. What about the nonhuman world? What are the layered weaves of interspecies communication? How, for instance, does a deer speak to us? Or a river? Or a sycamore?

When it comes to honeybees, communication cannot happen with words, barks, chirps, or tell-tale changes in the weather. The way the honeybee experiences the world through her senses is quite different than us. Her experience of color alone surpasses the human visual spectrum.

To learn to speak with bees we have to suspend our fixed version of reality and open to possibility. Act as if it is possible, and magic occurs.

I once asked the a colony of honeybees if I could open their hive up and show the interior of the hive to a group of students. I spoke words of love, and explained why I wanted to open the hive. I closed my eyes and waited. And then my mind was flooded with the sensation of purple. That is, if a color I've never seen before, a color suffused in emotion and texture, could be considered "purple."

With my waking eyes, I had never encountered such a color, but the closest description I can come up with was a soft, vibrant, electric, ecstatic purple. A violet hue that somehow conveyed pride, joy, and something ineffable in a momentary flash.

It was a warm day in February, a perfect time to check on how the bees fared through the cold winter months. To survive winter, bees have to amass and store enough honey, gathered from nectarous flowers, to feed the small overwintering bees. The ancient Greeks associated honey with ambrosia, the divine food of the gods. Priestesses associated with fertility, prophesy, and the mysteries of life and death were sometimes known as "bees," or Melissae.

Goddesses such as Demeter and Artemis were also given the title bees. The Ancient Greeks saw the bees themselves as messengers who could travel between the realms of human and gods, bearing their holy sacrament. Our tiny, veil-winged sisters depend on this honey through the cold months, when Persephone herself resides in the underworld, and nothing blooms above.

Well, not quite nothing. Here in Coastal California, the rosemary starts blooming in December. It was the rosemary the bees were talking about. Large dusty green bushes lined the edge of the apiary, tiny purple blooms flowing with nectar. Through sharing their experience of purpose, I somehow knew it was the rosemary. It was a taking of the hand:

"Here, come. We are so proud and excited to show you what we are doing."

In my time communicating with the bees, they've spoken to me in such a stunning variety of ways, I am often brought to my knees in humble reverence for who and what they are. In my hopes to understand them, I have engaged with practical, observational, and scientific knowledge. I understand the biological nature of a colony, what's happening at the entrance of a hive on any given day, or what different behaviors mean. I have also employed nonlinear pathways of knowledge: dreams, meditations, and intuition to take me to places intellectual knowledge cannot. It is here that the bees offer their golden threads of connection bridging my human perception with the absolutely bee-ness of bees.

Children are apt to believe they can speak to the nonhuman world around them. It comes naturally, and is a mix of the brilliance of the imagination, and some older, ancient inheritance that erodes away from us as we enter more fully into modern society. For some of us, the ability to speak with the plants, animals, and spirits is never lost. For many of us however, that intrinsic ability to speak to a tree, or see the fairies tending the wildflowers, turns into a longing to be able to do such things. That longing eventually matures into an adult heartache to be reunited with the vibrant sentience all around you. To have modern belief systems of dead matter and mountains devoid of soul are to be proved wrong. To reawaken a romance with the animate Earth. Driven by a belief that in fact it *is* possible (it must be!), we turn to earth-honoring cultures, myths, ancient ancestors, fairytales, art, and, of course, the imagination, looking for the way back to enchantment.

I can't tell you how long I've wanted to be able to see fairies or hear the stones. As an avid reader of mythic fiction, I had some rather short-sighted notions of what such encounters might be like. To begin with, I thought they would be magnificent moments of finally seeing something magical with my own two eyes. Some part of me hoped for a magical power to suddenly "turn on" within me, at which point I would be able to see, hear, and feel all I longed for. What happened instead was the slow development of trust between myself and my intuition. To become conversant with the trees, rivers, and spirits, we must first acquaint our intuitive self with our thinking self.

The other-than-human world is always speaking to us, and the tools we have to receive such communications are those we are born with: our bodies, our senses, and our imagination. To speak to the bees, or hear the language of the stars, we must first learn how such things are translated through our individual systems of knowing. This includes the agile, edge-walker skill of recognizing how and when the imaginal moves from "make believe" into "seeing true." This form of intuitive awareness is available to all of us, should we choose to explore its depths.

One of the places this can be most readily experienced is within the realm of dreams. However, to approach dreams as an avenue toward communication with the more-than-human world, we must first lean into the globally held indigenous knowledge that dreams are not just our subconscious processing our days and our life, but rather, an active and collective location that sits at the confluence of the imagination and spirit-world. Here, we are not dreaming alone, but dreaming within a greater weave. The weave or life on earth, made up of the individual dreams of all life on earth, woven into a tapestry. This continually unfolding work of the dreamer's art can be thoughtfully tended to by dreamers seeking to intentionally dream within the collective weave. That is to say to contribute to what ecologist Thomas Berry calls "the Dream of the Earth."

We alone are not responsible for the Dream of the Earth. We are active participants in the dreaming. We can join with bees, waterfalls, mycelia, and badgers to dream reality into being. To imagine what else is possible. Animist and author David Abrams writes: ". . . along with the other animals, the stones, the trees, and the clouds, we ourselves are characters within a huge story that is visibly unfolding all around us, participants within the vast imagination, or Dreaming, of the world."

When we dream, make art, dance, and "make-believe," we traverse the wondrous landscape of the imaginal, where possibilities hitherto blocked to our thinking mind, become ribboned pathways through the dark, opening to new vistas of living and relating. This courting and crafting of the imaginal is what all animistic cultures fluently practice as they encounter the more-than-human world.

If you can't hear the flowers speak, why not invite them to whisper their language into your dreams? If you can't see the water nymphs with your own two eyes, why not draw them, dance them, or imagine them to life within your being? At some point, you will cross the invisible bridge between "making it all up," and knowing that something—no—*someone* is most certainly having a conversation with you.

The first time I learned that I really could hear the bees was through a series of dreams. It was my first year beekeeping, and I was still in the early stages of learning what bees were all about. Honeybees are a superorganism, meaning that they are a group of individuals comprising a whole. A social unit that together, makes one organism. A single individual cannot survive without the whole.

In my early days of beekeeping, I saw the bees as a superorganism, but failed to understand how that organism is also the pliable, resonant beeswax, the movement of air and heat through the interior, or the thick scent-magic providing the bees with immune system support and a sense of belonging all at the same time. Nor did I fully grasp that the colony, as a whole, could speak to me. That it could reach out through the magnetic void between bee mind and human mind, and grab hold. You see, the bees sent me dreams.

In the spring of 2011, I caught a beautiful swarm of bees in an apple tree. A swarm is a how honeybees reproduce as a whole, providing a new colony, when the old colony splits in two. For thousands of years swarms in the spring have heralded abundance, good luck, and the blessing of the gods. They were so highly coveted and beloved in ancient Ireland that a series of bee laws were established to support the rules around which folk could collect swarms and house colonies.

As the season warmed, the young swarm, now a colony, began to expand, building beeswax comb and raising brood. Around midsummer, I began having nightmares about black widow spiders. The first dream was fairly tame, just some black widows on the ceiling. However, over the next two weeks, the dreams continued, every few nights. In each dream, the black widows became more frequent and closer to the ground. In the final dream, I was crawling on my belly through my basement, toward the beehive, with black widow web all around me, and spiders everywhere. There was hardly any space to move at all. I woke up in a cold sweat and instantly understood: there was a black widow in my bee hive.

I immediately donned my hat, veil, and gloves and headed for the hive. Sure enough, magnificently occupying the back third of the hive was a dazzlingly large black widow. As if to communicate her prowess, the desiccated body of a honey bee lay on the wood floor beneath her. However, what truly caught my breath was the comb. Bees live on beeswax comb. They make comb withtheir own bodies, shaping into the hexagonal structure we associate with honeycomb. However, not all comb is honeycomb. Much of the comb is actually dedicated to the brood rearing, and this is quite literally where the bees live. An indication of a healthy hive in the spring and summer is the sight of thousands of bees covering the comb. On this morning, the comb in the back of the hive was abandoned. The bees were crammed into the comb in the front of the hive, but the back of the hive was empty, silver shiny strands of widow web having taken over the nest. The bees were literally being crowded out by predatory web. Dream after dream, the space I could move in got smaller and more cramped. Day after day, the space the bees could inhabit in got smaller. They did not dare traverse the combs laced with web, or they would surely become ensnared. Yet, they needed that abandoned comb for survival. They needed the space to fill with pollen and nectar, or the bees would have nothing to feed their young, nor any stores of honey to get them through the winter dearth. The dreams were a cry for help. The bees blasted through my preconceived conceptions of what "communicating" with them might look like and got the message to me: "help us." It was in this moment that I shifted from being a beekeeper to being a bee guardian.

To be a bee guardian is to be consciously aware that we are both the watcher and the protector. We are witness to the sacred, and, as witness, we can also act as the keeper or care-taker who seeks to support the bees in their fullest expression of self. The bees are granted the right of sentience and sovereignty.

Some of this philosophy remains, albeit faintly, in the old folk tradition of Telling the Bees. Flourishing in the 19th century, the folk art of Telling the Bees can be found in Europe and the Americas, expressing itself most strongly in the UK and Ireland. Its roots can be traced back to the 16th century, and it is likely far older than that. In its simplest form, Telling the Bees is the act of literally going to one's bee hive or apiary (group of hives), and speaking in a low voice or whisper about recent major events such as births, deaths, travelers, and weddings.

With this tradition came a host of superstitions and practices indicating a level of respect and reverence for the "mind" of the bee colony that was not afforded to most animals or other aspects of nature at that time. It was believed that if a bee hive was not informed of the death of their beekeeper, they would abscond and fly away. In some regions, new babies were introduced to the hive, while in others a bride was tasked with walking her bridegroom by the hives to see if they approved of the match.

The practice was strongest when it came to deaths. The method of telling sometimes involved taking the house key, and knocking three times on the hive, then whispering the sad tidings to the bees, imploring them to stay.

This was well into the Christian Era, but the bees, once representing the Great Mother Goddess, were still seen as emissaries of the divine. In this case, they were regarded as messengers of Christ. What is fascinating, is that the awareness of bees as spirit allies endured past the systematic dismantling of pagan, animistic traditions.

There is an old Scottish adage, made popular by Fiona Macleod: "Ask the wild bees what the Druids knew." What indeed, did the honey bees store in the sacred tree hollows, held in each drop of honey, each golden grain of pollen? The ancient druids were the wise people of the Celtic nations, who held worship in sacred groves of trees, the natural habitat for wild bees. What, indeed, did the bees overhear? Could the folk traction of Telling the Bees point to an older understanding of turning to the natural world to both communicate and receive sacred knowledge?

Could we perhaps, approach the bee hive as a store house of wisdom? Keepers of sage council? And if so, how do we begin to access that wisdom? By humbly beginning to relate. By having a conversation, even it seems one sided at first.

What might you tell the bees of your heart today? What personal realizations have come to you this moon cycle? Can you show them your grief? Your worries? Can you sit by a hive and quiet your mind, offering the bees an introduction through words, mental visualizations, prayer, or even music?

Or, if you do not have a beehive nearby, can you go to trees, the bees' ancient home, and imagine a hive? Call up the spirit of the bees to be with you.

Perhaps you have a pressing decision and need some advice? Perhaps you have a question you've been chewing on for some time and want to see if the bees might offer their own pollinated insight?

Then begins the true magical act. To believe the bees can hear you. To believe the bees will answer you. To believe you will hear that answer. That is, to believe that you are an essential part of the dream weave. That you are wanted and welcomed into the weave between human and bee.

Get quiet, close your eyes, and listen with all of your senses opened. You too can hear like the fox. You too can see like the bee. You are one who swims like the serpent, who reads the messages of the wind like the falcon, who feels the stones in your bones and cosmos in your eyes. You are relevant and worthy of the direct, cryptic, and spiraling messages from the bees.

Taken by Faeries

BY AMANDA YATES GARCIA

A Trip To Grandmother's House

A few years ago, Papa—my step-grandfather—passed away. He'd taught me to ride a bike, slipped cookies in my lunch pails, and had called me Tiger. My grandmother was grieving; they'd been married for fifty years. I went to her house in the foothills outside of Sacramento to help her sort through his things and her grief. They'd lived in a Ranch-style house built in the 70s that smelled of medicine for the aged, with low ceilings, mirrored sliding doors on the closets, couches and chairs all facing a large flat screen TV in the living room. As a child, I'd been close to my grandparents. As I grew older, our relationship thinned and waned. They'd caught me "snuggling" with my best friend when I as fifteen. At thirty, they said the feminist "rants" I posted on Facebook were so emasculating it would keep me single. They didn't love it when I become a public witch, though they were impressed to see me on Tucker Carlson. Whenever they saw me, they always commented on my appearance positively or negatively, depending on which way the scale had tipped since I'd last seen them. Because of all these things and more, as I got older we struggled to find common ground. One of the last remaining ways my grandmother and I had found a way to connect was through our ancestors.

My grandmother was the only person in the family who still remembered anything about them. We liked to sit, her in her electric reclining chair, me on the sofa, going through boxes of old photos: Daguerreotypes from the 1800s with stoney faced couples in starched lace collars, and sticky 1980s snapshots of kids on water skis shot on disposable cameras. She'd tell me stories and

A CONFLUENCE OF WITCHES

I'd record them on my iPhone. I wanted to know the names of my ancestors. I wanted to visit their graves, to call upon them in ceremony when I needed wisdom or support. I wanted, somehow, at last, to feel less alone. Together, my grandmother and I dwelt in the period drama of my great-great-great grandfather arriving by clipper ship from England during the Gold Rush. We discussed our ancestors' lives on ranches, farming the sandy soil of Arroyo Grande, Atascadero, and the citrus groves of Orange County long before it was turned into a business park parking lot.

She told me of how when her father lost his ranch job during the Depression, the only job he could get was on one of the oil rigs they were building out in the Santa Barbara channel. The channel where the ancestors of the Chumash swam as dolphins, and their goddess, Hutash, had built the rainbow bridge.

"Did our ancestors have any dealings with the Indigenous people of California?" I asked her.

"They were around," she replied, which I took to mean that she didn't know, nor think about it much.

My grandmother told me how her father, Grandpa Bruce, had worked his way up, becoming an engineer during the oil boom, handing me a picture of a small shack in the middle of an oil field in Culver City, where he and my great-grandmother lived while he was working. Those oil rigs are still there, locusts sucking at the earth in what is now a mostly Black neighborhood, releasing benzene, hydrogen sulfide, and formaldehyde particulate matter into the air and soil where they cause depression, lung disease, and birth defects. I know exactly what toxins they release because of my activist work to get the rigs taken down. "Your great-grandfather built those." My grandmother beamed at me with pride, pointing to the picture.

As her story came to the 1950s, when my mother was born, I felt the haunting of our family ghosts, always lurking nearby, creep closer. Like Sarah Winchester, the widow of the Winchester Mystery House—where my grandmother had taken me as a child—who believed that the ghosts of all people who'd been killed by the Winchester rifle her husband had invented would haunt her until she was dead in the grave. My Papa had once been a prison guard at the California Men's Colony. Even forty years after he retired, the ghosts of the prisoners had followed him, peering through the windows at night, between the slats of the heating vents in the walls of their house. It's why he collected so many guns, had cameras set up everywhere. So many ghosts. It seemed that every member of my family had gathered some of their own. And that day I could feel them thicken the air, like the whine of the buzz-saw I could hear from the yard, as my Grandmother approached the horror of what she was about to say.

Fairies As Ancestors

In our colonial world, few remember the processes of ancestor veneration. In pre-modern Europe, there's a well-documented history that what we now call fairies were ancestral spirits, the spirits of those who were buried in the land, becoming part of the hidden springs, the crystal caves, the thickets of heather and gorse. Fairies were shape-shifting ecological beings and spirits of place. Sometimes, they were thought of as angels, other times devils. Over centuries, through the machinations of industrial capitalism—the enclosure of public lands, the forests destroyed to build naval ships, the persecution of those that knew the old ways—belief in those numinous land spirits waned, until the fairies diminished, becoming charming bedtime stories for children, or were forgotten entirely.

THE CHASM

Long ago, Grandma's story began, when my mother was twelve, and women couldn't have bank accounts or get credit cards, my biological grandfather—whom I never met—returned after six months in the psych ward. He'd been sent there after he'd exposed himself to a mother and daughter in the de

Young Museum; after that thing with the little girl next door and their late-night "flashlight game"; after the time when my uncle, age four, came toddling inside from the front yard with a note pinned to his romper, telling the "family of perverts" to get out of town. My grandfather had gotten off lightly with the psych ward instead of prison, because he was white, and middle class, and his brother was an attorney.

While he'd been gone, my grandmother, who had no credentials, no college, and no work experience, had managed to get a job selling ads at the *Pasadena Bee.* She went there in the day, leaving her children—my twelve year old mother, my eleven year old aunt, and my two uncles, ages eight and six at home alone with their father.

She left my twelve year old mother alone with her father. And when she came back, she discovered that he had done something horrible to her, an unimaginable thing. A thing that, when I heard it, made my palms clammy, my stomach cramp. My arm pits became sticky with the stench of adrenaline. Her story plunged me into a pit of guilt and self-loathing. My mother had always claimed she'd protected me from the worst of her childhood stories, but I hadn't felt protected. I'd never felt protected from the horror of my family. I'd felt steeped in it. Tarnished by it. Bitter about how the violence had just gone on and on and on and that we all got tangled in it and implicated somehow. I was angry with my mother, because she'd lived in a land of ghosts and didn't seem to want to leave (and maybe she *couldn't* leave or didn't know how). I could see her across the chasm. I called out to her, but we could never really touch. So my teenage solution was to roll my eyes when she recited the sagas of her childhood traumas, because they seemed like an excuse for all the ways I'd felt alone in my childhood, and because they were mixed in with the collective toxins of our violent history as colonizers, seeping out beyond our family into the groundwater of our nation, where everyone had been defiled by it. During her childhood, my beautiful mother, her wings clipped, became inaccessible to me, and maybe to everyone. My mother had always said she hadn't told me everything—and on that day at my grandmother's house, I found out it was true.

The Western Lands

When the Romans came to the isles of Britannia in ever escalating waves of violence, they burned down the sacred groves wherein dwelled the ancestral land spirits. They dragged their iron plow through the soil, where the people of the land had poured their blood to ensure fertility, and where on windy nights the corn wolf bristled beneath the harvest moon. The plow disrupted root systems, overexposing microorganisms, degrading the richness of the land, forcing it to over-produce. It was then that the power of the hidden people began to diminish. The faerie folk were said to leave those isles then, sailing west, to the land of the dead. Which also happens to be the direction in which many of us were born.

A DANCE AROUND THE BONFIRE

After my grandmother told me about the horrible thing my grandfather did, which I won't say, because I want to spare you having it branded into your mind as it is into mine, I ran out into a yard choked with gasoline smoke and ashes. I ran out into the a whirlwind of blades ripping through the flesh of trees, and the ratcheting of metal on wood thumping against my chest. My uncle, the one who'd had pervert pinned to his romper, the one who'd been dropped into the bathtub by his ankles and rescued by my ten year old mother, my now sixty year old uncle with a series of wives from developing nations — the current one being younger than his twenty-three year old daughter—was directing a crew of migrant laborers to rip out the manzanita gathering in thickets with the scrub oak and the juniper brush and toss it onto a pyre at the center of the yard. Meanwhile he rode—like a child imitating a cowboy at a rodeo, with that kind of seriousness and pride—a tractor all around the yard, mowing back and forth over the mounds, all flattened now, ripped raw and denuded. These thickets were home to voles, mule deer and field mice, yellow-bellied marmot, red-breasted robin and tiny flammulated owls, not to mention the plants themselves. The coyote bush, the ash, the buckeye and coffeeberry. Lace lichens, turkey tail mushrooms, split gill fungi that can open and close at will.

My uncle joined me where I stood by the fire, stiff as an arrow shot in spite. It felt like the saws were cutting into my own body, or at least into someone I loved. Someone I couldn't protect. Jovially, my uncle told me not to worry, and clapped a hand on my shoulder. What he was doing was good for the land. When he was done it would look like a city park. "You know the kind," he said, "with picnic tables and bar-b-cues and all the grass." What he was doing was good for the oak trees, he said as he tossed a branch of California hazelnut into the bonfire. This way all the other plants wouldn't crowd them and take their water. He pulled out his phone and scrolled through websites, saying, "Look here, see!" while I fumed. It's not *that* bad, he seemed to be saying. Nothing is ever *that* bad.

"That website was probably commissioned by Exxon Mobile," I responded.

"You're being a pain in the ass," he replied with a wounded look. "You used be so sweet when you were a child. What happened to that little girl?"

Sacred Burns

This is a land that knows fire. The Nisenan, Maidu, and Miwok people, who numbered in the tens of thousands here less than eight generations ago, practiced sacred burns. Fire was a way of honoring and tending the land, making sure the deer and all the other creatures had enough to eat, and that the future fires wouldn't burn so hot that roots would be destroyed. Families came together for the burns. Everyone in the village had to agree, "this is the time." Elders and children. There could be no one who had doubts, no one who worried that it wasn't the right time, or that the trees or the animal kin couldn't take it. Before the burning began, they would bless the land, then gather the best and straightest branches of hazel to use for baskets. Rather than fighting the fire, they worked with it. The plants, the fire, the land itself were all sacred and the burning was done in ceremony. When Western settlers arrived, they forced the Maidu people off their land, put a bounty on their heads in an explicitly stated intention to exterminate them. They banned all sacred ceremonies, including controlled burns, which eventually led to the uncontrollable fires we see today.

TREE FRIEND

I surveyed the fragments of surviving thicket. Acres of it would soon be gone. And yet there it stood, creating a world where trust seemed possible, where kinship still lived, contiguous with my world of ghosts and betrayal. My uncle, incapable of tolerating anyone's disapproval, again directed me to the authority of his phone, "See this here," he said, pointing to a green blob on Google Maps. "See that green part going from Grandma's property all the way down the hill? What's going to happen when that catches fire? A fire would rip through that so fast. Before your eighty-nine-year-old grandmother could even get out of her chair." My grandmother could barely walk because of the polio she'd had as a child. She needed help to go to the bathroom, much less to get in her car. "When all that catches on fire, which it eventually will, do you want your eighty-nine-year-old grandmother to be burned alive? Do you?"

I stood in silence, not relishing the idea of my eighty-nine-year-old grandmother burning alive, but neither ready to concede. My grandmother had hired "Tree Friend" to come rip out the thicket. "But the field mice in their dens will be ground up," I'd said as the stump grinders began that morning. The California Quail, a species known for their strong family bonds, would stop their cooing and watch from the upper branches of the oak tree as the nests they'd built in the scrub, and their pointy speckled eggs that had yet to hatch, and the hatchlings themselves, were chucked into the bonfire. Ecosystems work collaboratively. When thickets like this are destroyed, whole ecosystems collapse with them. My grandmother had said I sounded like one of those environmentalists. People "who get in the way of good jobs," all because of the owls. "Well, I don't care about owls," she'd scoffed, as if I'd told her she shouldn't clear her yard because of the fairies.

I was speechless. Powerless. What could I do? How could anyone not care about owls?

My grandmother wanted me to know she loved the land. That's why she moved out here. What they were doing was an improvement. She wanted me to come back to her side; I know she was lonely too. She tried to comfort me. But I could not be comforted. Extracting the life from the land was not an improvement.

Later, outside, I asked my uncle. "Why do people move to the woods if they just want to chop it all down?"

"It has to go," he said testily. "The insurance people are going to come out here and check. They already told us they wouldn't insure a place with all this bio mass on it. No insurance, no house." Maybe it feels easier not to see wrongs if there's nothing you can do about them. Though, from a less generous perspective, the property would also be his one day. There was no way he was going to lose it because of some random burrowing owls.

The law of insurance had decreed: the *bio mass* must be destroyed.

Dancing around the Sacred Tree

Throughout the classical world it was well known that the pagans of Northern Europe worshiped in groves of trees, and worshiped even the trees themselves. The rituals of the ancient Celtic priests and political leaders, the Druids, took place in sacred groves centering around an oak tree. In the 1st century A.D., Roman general Gaius Suetonius Paulinus ordered the destruction of the sacred groves on the island of Mona, the center of druidic power and religious activity, capturing or killing all who defended them. Later, after the conquest of the Holy Roman Empire was complete in Britain, in an effort to enforce Christianity,

King Cnut, in his Constitution *of the 11th century, forbid the common folk still practicing the old ways from worship of idols or heathen gods, or "the sun or the moon, fire or rivers, water-wells or stones, or forest trees of any kind." Tacitus explicitly describes how the Romans targeted the sacred groves of the Germanic tribes as part of their campaign to suppress their religion and culture.*

The Germanic tribes believed that the first people, Ash and Embla, came from the trees, and in fact that the trees were gods, and had created humans in the first place. When people died, they were often buried in hollowed-out trees where they merged back in with the forest to become the ancestors. The foremost symbol of the tribes was Irminsul, the world tree, which united heaven and earth, and in which all beings lived, and which stood as an actual tree, or a pole symbolizing a tree, a sacred gathering point for worship. The Frankish king Charlemagne cut Irminsul down, and after a series of battles which left thousands dead, or displaced from their homes and weak from famine and disease. The Saxons were forced to convert to Christianity in the mid-8th century A.D.. Later, in the medieval period, witches were said to dance around trees, harkening to a connection with their Pagan roots, and indeed that act continued in the form of dances around a Maypole festooned with flowers and wish ribbons, until that too was banned for a time in 1644. Soon after that, with Christianity firmly established, at the beginning of the colonial period, the British took control of Ireland, and over centuries deforested the entire island in order to claim the wood for the British naval ships; and to claim forest land for agriculture—despite, or perhaps because of, the fact that the indigenous Irish held the forests to be sacred land; and also in order to root out the Irish rebels, who often took shelter in the forests to engage in their acts of resistance. After the total conquest of pagan Europe, the colonial project went on to begin the process of colonization and deforestation in the "New World" and around the globe.

ENTERING THE FAIRY CIRCLE

Leaving my uncle at the bonfire, I dashed across the meadow and scrambled through barbed wire into what remained of the thicket, an acre or two, dense and pathless. I traveled prostrate on my knees, through dirt and leaves, brambles grasping at my clothes and hair, sharp little fangs of oak leaves nipping into my palms. A loneliness inside ripped through me like a stone. To be close is to know the inner world of the other. My family had never known my inner world, didn't want to, maybe couldn't, and I had never known theirs. Home is somewhere you're always welcome. Had I ever been home? Was it even possible to be welcome in a land that had never invited you in and probably didn't want any of your kind to be there?

I lay down in the dirt in a space just big enough for a clan of deer. What magic could I practice here? If magic is the art of transforming reality according to your will, I knew that my magic would fail here, was already failing. Nothing about the destruction of this thicket was going to go according to my will. If I couldn't offer my magic, my first thought was to give the land what I'd always wanted instead. But what had I always wanted? Safety? I couldn't give the land safety. I searched for something equally valuable I could offer. I could give the land kinship. I could see it and hear it and be curious about its inner world. I could ask to know it, and listen for its answer. I could love it so much that its pain was my pain. Even if I couldn't make the pain stop I could be its witness, I could let the hurt of it roll through me instead of pretending it wasn't there.

I whispered, so that my lips kissed the damp earth and I tasted the loam and moss of it, "I'm sorry. I'm with you. I'm yours. I'm sorry." I pressed my forehead and palms to the ground, let my pulse become one with the sap of the life force as it pulsed through us all.

On my closed eyelids I could feel the air shifting, alive with presence. Could I sleep there, I wondered? A net of shadows rippled above me. Opening my eyes, I saw that nothing had changed but the light. Golden rays glittering through a canopy of sycamore and madrone. Leaves rustling, twigs cracking, the slow chill of the autumn lacing through the wind. I sensed that someone was there. Groggily, I pushed myself up. No humans were present. I was alone with the scrub oak and the wolf spiders. Near my hands, half buried, a pair of antlers broke through the surface of the earth.

There were two of them, they must have been shed at different times. One antler was ancient, bleached, swollen with time and rough as unfinished wood.

The other was smooth as a sapling, younger, fresh, and mossy green around the base. Male mule deer get their name from their big ears. They have black on their tails as if they've been dipped in paint, and they drop their antlers every year. Dusk dwellers, crepuscular beings, these deer rest in the day and hide at night, but come out into the fields through the swirling mists of twilight to feast on the damp sedge grass. They snuffle through meadows for thimbleberries and shoots of willow, then pronk, all four limbs leaving the ground, up and down through the brambles on their way down the hill to the pond.

I was alone with the King of the Fairies. Arawn, Arawn was near.

The King of the Fairies

The White Hart, the stag, is an animal avatar of Arawn, lord of the faeries, and exemplar of their power, who is sometimes known to claim human helpers. In the Welsh tale of the Mabinogion, he is guardian of the forest, a protector, a guide, a psychopomp who can travel between worlds. A god of justice, he appears when boundaries have been transgressed, warning of the consequences of human violations and betrayals. He appears in liminal places, crossroads, beyond hedges, at hollow hills and sacred circles, places where worlds come together and bleed into one another. Sometimes, if one is lucky, humble, and a friend to the faeries, if one seeks to live in harmony with life, protect it, care for it, nurture it, and love it like family and be loved by it in return, Arawn will appear to that person as a blessing. If one meets the King of the Fairies, they become Fairie-led and Fairie-friended, bonded to the spirits of the land forevermore. Is it possible that the White Hart of the faeries, and the Choi-Yek'-Ke, the Black Tail Deer of the Miwok people, can co-exist in peace? If we approach them with respect, perhaps the deer will guide us into the realms of enchantment where all beings are connected.

A CONFLUENCE OF WITCHES

THE ENERGY MOVES THROUGH US

Night fell. All the workers had gone home for the day. The deer returned from their daily sojourns to a smoldering land. I returned to the house to find my grandmother and uncle sitting on the couch watching FOX News.

Scurrying to protect the holy horns from their sight, I tried to dart into my room up the hall. They called out to me, "What's that you've got there?"

I paused, shrugging, and mumbled, "Antlers."

"You just *found* those?" they asked, incredulous.

I pressed the antlers to my chest like a cross holding the promise of redemption. My family could've borne them too if only they'd been paying attention. But had I arrived only a few days later, the antlers would've been ground up by tractors and burned, the deer that made their home in that thicket dispossessed and chased away, given over to the wasting disease.

"They come from Grandma and Papa's house, they have our energy in them," my grandmother said, uncharacteristically. She was not a deeply spiritual person. Though she did love the deer. She watched them every morning in the meadow from her kitchen window and would text me about their movements. But she wasn't one to talk about "energy." Even though she didn't go to church, she was Christian, in the sense that, well, she said she was, and she thought anybody who didn't say they were had something wrong with them. "Now you have our energy to take with you wherever you go," she smiled at me.

My heart said no. *No!* Even if I was tarnished with the perversions of my bloodline, I wanted the antlers to belong to the faerie realm. Out loud I said nothing. Half smiled. Went to my room. There I kneeled and prayed that the antlers keep the energy of the deer, the burrowing owls, and the split gill fungi whose spores I invited to blossom in me and show me how to belong, and how to honor the belonging of others. I welcomed the spores into my heart and mind. May they take root in me. May they fruit and decay in me. May they eat away my corruption and feed others from my body. May my body be a site of mushroom led blood and soil toxic waste remediation.

Fire as Kin, Land as Kin

The Miwok have never entirely abandoned their sacred burns, though the settlers continue to punish them for it. Some elders say the Maidu speakers were born of fire, and dependent upon it still. Yet, now, because the settler practices of fire suppression have caused so much harm, the wildfires have become so apocalyptic that fire fighters are turning to the First Nations—whose apocalypse arrived hundreds of years ago with the settlers—to ask them for advice. Now the Miwok and other First Nations are at the forefront of the move to ecological wellbeing. Burns in these lands should be led by indigenous people. Fire clearing is not a violation, the violation is the land being treated as an object, "a resource," devoid of feeling, to be managed, rather than loved. Only when the land is treated as sacred, only when we recognize all as kin, will the apocalypse of our loneliness end.

BONES ARE SACRED OBJECTS

I left the next morning and drove through the foothills to Highway 50, through a land of wineries and wedding estates, past Green Valley Ranch and Blue Water Farms, and I noticed. . . all the properties had been cleared. It's just oak trees and grass now. City parks and bar-b-cues for hundreds of miles. As if thickets had never been there at all.

If I looked closely I could still find a few pockets of refuge, slivers of unincorporated land with patches of gooseberry and lilac, dogwood and sagebrush, where sedge and split gill mushrooms still grow, sending their spores into new hosts, catching them in their fairy circles, inoculating them with their kinship.

FOR THE FAIRIE LED

Once you are faerie-led, you can never go back. Once you have been taken by fairies, everywhere you go, there is kin. You've been given a gift by mysterious forces who expect something from you in return. Their gift economy is a web of bonds, a web of kinship. You are bound now, to make a sacrifice, to pay respect. You are bound in a reciprocity, an embeddedness, from which you cannot, and will never want to, leave. The otherworld is the inner world of the earth. Your inner world and the otherworld are one.

PLACE THE OFFERING AT THE CROSSROADS

Arriving home in Los Angeles, I placed the antlers on my altar. These bones are sacred objects, now they collaborate with me for my spells. Antlers offer protection; the deer grow them to assert their will. They are my magical tools, and I aim to be their tool in return. I hold them and they hold me. As wands I wield them, and in turn they wield me. A wand is a tool for focusing energy, for directing transformation. As staffs the antlers support and guide me, as their staff I offer them my support and willingness to guide others toward their faerie circle in return.

The witch's body is the crossroads, the place where all worlds meet. Would Arawn have traveled through if I had not been there to witness his presence, to remember his connection to the deer of Annwn? White Hart meets white-ness, my finger slides down the rough edge of a bone-white antler, telling me how to work with the energy. How do I let the enchanted land sing out through me? What is it the owls want to make known?

CHAPTER 6

HEALING PATHWAYS

Spells & Meditations on
Healing Work

HEALING HAS ALWAYS BEEN THE CENTRAL duty of the witch. Whether they hold the power to journey and collect directives from the spirit realm on how to heal individuals, or they are the keepers of nourishing family recipes, witches have many methodologies for activating healing for individuals and for communities. Modern witches find themselves holding both ancestral healing knowledge, as well as navigating relatively new ailments; combating the side effects of alienation, the destructive by-products of capitalism, or the basic overstimulation we all feel living in this modern world.

While there are countless spells and practices that promise healing, it is ever important to remember that healing is no singular event. Healing is a spiralic endeavor, with many peaks and valleys. Healing can be both painful and blissful, cathartic and quiet. One would like to think that healing feels like a day at the spa, but the reality is that the cure can often be more painful than the symptoms of the illness. Witches are uniquely suited for this type of energetic work, because we are not afraid of the shadow, we are not afraid to venture through the dark wood in order to find the treasure. Oftentimes those shadowy places in ourselves are the places where the medicine hides.

Many folks discover witchcraft as part of their spiralic healing path. As witches endeavor on their own healing journeys, their practices become deeply embedded into their psyches, their spirits, and to their relationships. Healing modalities include working with plant medicines, herbalism, dreaming, energy work, laying of hands, performing cleansings, mediumship, divination, and many many others. Some witches' healing experiences are so profound that they become inspired to offer spiritual healing services to support others along their healing paths.

The term "healer" is a title to treat cautiously, for it certainly has its shadow. When working with a self-proclaimed healer, some are tempted to relinquish their power to that individual, trusting too readily and giving their power away in the hopes of being "fixed" or "healed" in the passive sense. However, healing is a process of shared responsibility, not one that can be solely facilitated by a practitioner without any collaboration from the individual wishing to be healed. Ultimately, healing is a community project and is never finished.

There is no ultimate healing experience. Each one of us wanders through the world with the potential to heal, and it takes a series of often cyclical experiences to tune into the texture of your healing process. Sometimes the spontaneous reading of a poem sparks an awakening to a hidden and tender part of the psyche. The scent of a rose can crack us open. There is no telling when we are ready to receive healing, or what might catalyze a healing experience.

As modern witches, it is important that we tread the well worn labyrinth of healing with care, authenticity, and reverence. Give thanks to the healers who you choose to collaborate with. Offer blessings to the plants that so generously share their energetic teachings with us. Remember to feed the spirits who guide and compassionately protect you. These meditations on healing are recipes to uplift, poems to inspire, and ethical guideposts to support you on your healing journey.

—Casey

Sacred Rose Healing

BY ALEJANDRA LUISA LEÓN

Roses began to show themselves to me prominently when I was grieving my father's passing. I began collaging found paper images at that time, and noticed that roses were popping up over and over again. Soon this became a theme, which is why it is so prominent in my artwork.

I connected the dots by remembering that my grandmother loved roses and had many rose patterned things. My mother, when reclaiming her independence, chose my grandmother's maiden name of Rose as her surname. It became clear that roses were my plant ally, and I began to work with them in the form of potions, bath rituals, aromatherapy, perfume, and in my magic practice. Any time I did, I found that not only would my heart open, but I would magnetize more abundance, pleasure, beauty, and love into my life.

In fact, the results were always so pleasing, that I began telling clients that when in doubt as to which color, stone, plant, or ritual to practice to solve their current issue, use love themes: pink candles, rose oil/essence/potion, rose quartz, etc. This is because you can't go wrong with healing your heart. So many issues stem from blockages in this area. I am quite fond of bath rituals, and find the following one to be quite effective. You can use it anytime to increase the energy of love in your life. By this I don't necessarily mean romantic. I mean that Venusian energy that makes everything in life feel kissed by roses. The most important place to begin is with self-love.

Sacred Rose Self-Love Bath Ritual

YOU WILL NEED:

- Beeswax, white, or pink candle

- Athame or other convenient scribing tool (safety pins work!)

- Rose, frankincense, or chosen incense (if you are sensitive and would rather not use smoke, omit this)

- Herbal tea of dried rose petals or buds

- Fresh rose petals

- Sea Salt

- Essential oil of rose absolute or rose geranium

- Rose quartz

- Self-love song or playlist if desired

Make a cup of rose tea. Take the tea and all of the ingredients to the tub with you. Turn on your ritual music if that will help you get deeper into this experience.

Take your candle, and with your scribing tool carve out the words "self-love" into your candle. If using a glass pillar, carve it at the top of the candle. If using a candle without glass, scribe it anywhere you like. Take the essential oil and anoint your candle. Work the oil toward you, along the entire length of the candle. If using a glass pillar, simply rub the oil on the exposed wax. Light your incense and the candle, and speak your intention for self-love out loud. You can put out your incense if it is going to become too intense for the entire bath ritual, or let it burn. Your choice.

Draw a bath. Put a couple of handfuls of sea-salt into the bath and swish it around to help it disintegrate. Place your crystal in the bath and climb in.

Have your tea nearby. Put three drops of the essential oil into your bath, along with the fresh rose petals. Give thanks to the spirit of the rose, and all of your tools, for assisting you in this ritual, and with your intention.

Once in your bath, lay back and relax. Take three deep inhalations and exhalations to release any tension. Grab your tea, close your eyes and completely immerse yourself in the sensations. Sip your tea. Smell the essential oils. Enjoy the heat of the water. Listen to the sounds of silence or music. Go deep. Know that you are steeping yourself in your intention to increase the love and appreciation you have for yourself. If you can, remain in this state for fifteen to twenty minutes. If you like your baths hot, then enjoy sweating as a way to release. Any time difficult emotions come up, do some deep exhalations out of the mouth. If you have an emotional release, that is okay. If you feel blissful, great. Whatever comes up is right for you.

When you are ready to finish, drain the tub. Stay in until the water drains out, knowing that the water is carrying off anything you needed to let go of. Let your candle burn out if you can. If you have to leave before the candle has burned to completion, put it out and light it when you return. Take the fresh rose petals and compost them in a garden or park if you can, rather than throwing them in the trash.

. . . .

You can do this ritual as often as you like, whenever you like, when you feel that you need that dose of love magic in your life.

Enjoy, and Blessed Be! xo

You're Reading Everyone around You, All the Time

Learning Energetic Boundaries with the Self and Others, for Readers, Healers, and Witches

BY RACHEL HOWE

Ethics are personal. They are not rules imposed; they are lines drawn and redrawn through experience. They come into being as manifestations of lessons learned, and intuitions listened to.

Once ethics are in place, they become values and roots. You don't have to keep thinking about them, because they become a natural part of you. These are not walls and boundaries that you have to keep reinforcing, they are organic limits of your holistic form that complement the ideal shape of yourself. Personal ethics are supportive and flexible guides and tools to use when making decisions that are healthy for you.

The worlds of magic, energy, and spirit are ones that we can enter at any time, but how we approach them determines our experiences there. If we have a strong ethical root system in place when working with others — other people, energies, or worlds — we are more likely to have a profound and meaningful interaction, without any level of harm done. Our personal Witch ethics modulate and inform our thoughts, feelings and actions, and in turn these thoughts, feelings and actions shape our realities. When we proceed without first consciously choosing and embodying our own values and beliefs, we can create unnecessary struggle for ourselves and others.

Foundational to a basis of witchcraft is an acceptance of the power of our own actions and behaviors, and the responsibility that goes along with this acknowledgement of personal power. Our own actions are what can most strongly shape and shift the world around us, for each of us. Our responsibilities include knowing that a single action on our part will be reflected back to us three times over, and acting accordingly. Among the many possibilities of the origin of the words "witchcraft" and "Wicca," one that I like descends from a word for "bend" ("wic" or "weik"). "According to this view, a Witch would be a woman (or man) skilled in the craft of shaping, bending, and changing reality." (Adler, Margot. *Drawing Down the Moon.* Boston: Beacon Press, 1986.)

When looked at from this perspective, the boundaries that can help us the most are actually the ones that are in regards to ourselves. We can be more effective in how we shape the world around us when we focus on our own thoughts and actions, not those of others. Everything is reflected from us and through us. We are not just singular beings, but a part of a larger web of existence. Because of this interconnected understanding of reality, focusing on ourselves doesn't create a vacuum or a bubble, but simply places our attention where it can be most effective, while still interacting within the larger web. When we heal ourselves, we heal everything. When we establish our own personal Witch ethics and maintain them as yet another living system within us, we demonstrate the possibility of this to others. Our personal Witch ethics in action are in and of themselves a form of healing.

The Witch, in historical mythology, is one who helps others while maintaining their emotional distance, and this distance is what creates historical discomfort in more capitalistic, authoritarian, patriarchal societies. The Witch says, "*I will give you my all for a specific purpose, but I will not fix you or do the work for you,*" and "*I will not compromise my own ethical code for your needs.*" "*I will stay true to a power that is beyond human, a power that is earth, sky, and spirit, and if your needs contradict these powers, I can't help you.*" This is uncomfortable for those who don't understand the deeper connection behind the ethics, or whose own ethics can be influenced by short-term needs. Modern Witches are in a unique position today, where there is less ostracization and more openness from mainstream society, and therefore more opportunity for the Witch to share their tools outside of their circle. Boundary work is a vital piece of this toolbox, in order to maintain a level of ethics that honors the Witch's values.

Early on in my own journey as a Tarot reader, and as a person in the midst of healing many of my own interpersonal dynamics, I met with a clairvoyant Tarot reader for a session. I told her I was also a reader, and so she put the cards aside and just channeled directly for me. In that moment I remember feeling validated as a peer, as one who also understood the invisible world. During our session she observed, not unkindly, "You're reading everyone around you, all the time. In fact, you're trying to read me right now."

I told her I didn't think I was, and we kept talking, but later upon reflection, I realized that I was, and that this habit was actually causing a lot of problems for me. When reading everyone around me, even when it was unnecessary and almost absurd—like when I am literally paying someone else to read me—I was accepting more work than I could handle. This insight sent me on a path of prioritizing boundary work in my own intuitive work, and somehow instantly ended my practice of reading everyone, all the time. Perhaps it was the acknowledgement: when we become conscious of something, we can suddenly make choices about it that we are unable to do when unconscious of it. Validation and compassionate acceptance of a behavior (being witnessed and loved) can negate the need for that behavior at all, enabling us to quickly release an unnecessary habit.

My impulse to read people all the time, unintentionally and outside of my professional reading work, was also a trauma response, a way to stay vigilant to manage other people's emotions so that I felt safe. My wounds and my gifts overlapped in such a way that I was going through life working as a reader at all times, even while outside of the container of a session, even outside of any useful function for my gift. The more my wounds heal, the less I need to use my gift for protection, and the more I can use it in the way it naturally wants to be used.

Whether you grew up intuitively reading the energy and feelings of others, or this skill was unlocked later in life, learning the healing modalities that use this type of intuitive reception in a focused and altruistic way can be profoundly validating. Randomly picking up on the emotions of others—peeking behind the curtain into a private inner dimension of reality instead of relying solely on what is shown and performed on stage—can disrupt our sense of clarity. It can be confusing to process the disconnect between unspoken felt truths and established external narratives. A professional intuitive or energetic reader can overcome this disconnect and direct their insight into wisdom that can help others to find peace, while also maintaining the peace of the reader.

However, there are very few guidelines in place to assist the reader as they navigate the waters of intuitive insight. This type of knowledge is usually passed down among families, lineages, mentors, or other closed systems. It is highly individualistic, which leaves a lot of freedom for the practitioner, as well as a lot of open-ended answers to any questions a student might have. Finding your own voice within these modalities is encouraged, and therefore there aren't many rules of engagement. More recently, trauma-informed practices have been incorporated into all kinds of healing work, including more traditional modes like counseling and psychotherapy, but often in more spiritual modalities, this has been less of a priority. When we are offering something that is desirable because of its difference from the mainstream or traditional status quo, we might throw out those more traditional rules in order to maintain that angle of difference.

We, and our clients, often want to be shown hard truths, or thrown into intense experiences in order to hasten the deeper and darker healing work.

There are ways to reconcile the special qualities of more esoteric healing work with the guidelines of a trauma-informed practice that don't have to conflict with the spiritual nature of esoteric work. In fact, the spiritual nature of esoteric work demands that we engage with clients in ways that are respectful, compassionate, generous, and careful.

When we start to awaken to our own power to sense what is beyond the standard five senses, we are opening up portals into the deeper nature of ourselves and of other realities. Entering these portals requires that we expand our understanding of what it means to sense, intuit, synthesize and translate information outside of established norms. We need to actually learn the language of our own intuition, not just to understand the meaning, but also the purpose. Every message we intuit has meaning; it contains both the information and a purpose, which leads to the action desired for the message. As healers and witches, we need to move through the initial magic trick of gleaning information, and move into the sense of purpose about what this information is for. In order to do this, we need to step outside our individual selves, and into the collective energy. Knowledge is transformed into wisdom by translating insights in such a way that it honors the self, honors the recipient, and honors the nature of the universe, which can sometimes exist beyond our realm of understanding.

When we think of boundaries, we might first think of the choices we make to keep the behavior of others from affecting us in undesired ways. We might think of boundaries that separate or create distance between ourselves and others, or ways to protect ourselves from others. By coming instead to a sense of boundary based more on what we want to happen rather than what we don't want to happen, we can flip the narrative of our own empowerment and desire.

Boundary work and personal Witch ethics spans the micro to the macro, the personal to the global, and can include:

- How we use language.

- How we engage with and respect timing and timelines in life.

- How we understand and conceptualize energy and the uses of it as it moves between people.

- Empathy as a tool.

- The borders of cultural lineages, and respecting closed practices.

Language

We can think about how we use language to communicate not just ideas and concepts, but emotional support. We often hear the term "holding space," and how we use language is a big part of holding space—or in other words, giving our client or friend permission to explore their own emotions, without fear of affecting ours. The language that gives this permission communicates safety to the client even when talking about difficult things, and assures the client that the practitioner is in command of their own safety, and so the client doesn't need to perform in any specific way to care-take the practitioner.

Timing

When we think of timing, we may think in terms of five-year plans or ten-year plans. We may decide we want certain things to happen in our lives at certain times, which creates a sense of urgency. Alternatively, if we surrender to a universal timeline, life events happen when it is best for the larger web of humanity, not for a single person. This acknowledges that we are existing not just as individuals, but as participants in a communal experience. It acknowledges that we are influenced by things (people, events, energy) that we don't yet have awareness of, and allows us to trust these mysterious forces as being positive and supportive, instead of assuming, and fearing, their destructive potential.

Energy

Working as a reader of energy requires that we each come to a personal definition of what Energy is, what its purpose and function is, and how we understand it to act, within the realm of our personal conceptions. Meaning, we can each learn the language, motion, sense and feeling, and motivation of energy as we personally interact with it. We can bring an intentional, intellectual understanding of energy as it relates to our cultural, historical, and religious backgrounds and interests. We can also bring an embodied understanding of how we have experienced energy in our own lives. And we can synthesize these concepts together until we feel we have a rooted and substantive grasp on the wisdom of energy as it relates to our personal experiences, and how it integrates into the larger webs we exist within, whether these are social, cultural, professional, familial, national, etc.

Empathy

Once we have a firm connection between ourselves and how we holistically relate to energy and its purpose in our lives, it becomes easy to extend this same depth to those around you. In this way, as practitioners, it can be easy to automatically offer compassionate generosity to your clients, without denying them their own agency in how they relate to energy in their lives. Because so much of empathic, intuitive wisdom is learned the hard way, by learning from crossing boundaries in our personal lives—our own boundaries or those of others—we need to consciously differentiate between empathy, sympathy, and empathic energy. If we mistake sympathy for empathy, we might fall into the common traps we see in "wellness" today: the bypassing of valid societal concerns, appropriation and cherry-picking of cultural practices, elevation of the guru, etc.

Empathy implies that we feel for someone as if they were us, and being empathic means that we can automatically feel the emotions of others as if they were ours. Sympathy implies that there is a separation or a distance between me and you, and implies a hierarchy or privilege—the one feeling sympathy is protected from experiencing the real feelings involved. When we are feeling empathy, we are able to see another person in as large and complex a dimension as we see ourselves, and we can extend the same respect and offer the same empowerment that we would want for ourselves. We don't seek to fix or change anyone, instead we afford them the same latitude of time and space that we would want for ourselves when we experience hardship. This is the purpose of empathy, to learn how to care for others the way we want to be cared for, which means respecting and responding to the boundaries of others, even if we don't understand them and even when they are different from our own.

Cultural borders

Empathy when working out the borders of cultural spiritual practices, when discerning where these borders do and don't overlap with our own lineages and practices, looks like offering that same wide latitude for the experiences of others to include things that we don't understand and don't involve us. Zooming out to see the entire web instead of our small single perspectives allows us to understand that there is so much we can't know, and to accept this as a neutral fact of reality rather than a judgment about us. For anyone who doesn't belong to a clear, established lineage of healing or spiritual work, there is still plenty of insight and guidance to be found throughout life, by observing the self through loving eyes.

Planetary Hours & the Doomsday Clock

On Being Sick & Carrying an Earth-Based Tradition in a Time of Ecological Calamity

BY OLIVIA PEPPER

Writer's notes:

I was punishingly, unbelievably late in submitting my piece for inclusion within this anthology. During the assembly process, my chronic health conditions flared/deepened and rendered me to near bedboundness for actual months upon months, my blood oxygen level consistently hovering around 91%, often accidentally drifting into sleep or the flickering realm of migraine, and while my rural internet faltered and my computer crashed, while I lost income from the writer's strike, while my mental health sputtered along, with my extremely limited resources I worked on compiling this piece.

As I finalized my work, multiple wars were in process around the world and my ability to focus was next to nil. It was finally the end of the hottest summer ever measured on Earth, with the month of July 2023 estimated to be the hottest in 120,000 years, and the monsoons we prayed for in my bioregion did not come. Wildfire smoke and/or floodwaters had blanketed much of the country for weeks on end; the place I was born was once again aflame. On stolen Chihene Nde land in so-called New Mexico, I performed my little rituals and at night read an old favorite from childhood: John Bellairs's *The House with a Clock in its Walls.*

This story is about a lonesome orphan taken in by his uncle, who turns out to be a wizard in what can be interpreted as a queerplatonic life partnership with a witch, Mrs. Zimmermann, who lives next door. Set in the 1940s, the story involves Lewis Barnavelt, the main character, clumsily dabbling in magic to impress a friend and making a mistake that sets into motion an accursed spellcraft that involves a doomsday clock hidden within the walls of their shared home. The book's denouement has the makeshift little family defeating the ghosts of the evil sorcerers who originally created the clock and plotted to bring about the end of the world through their own resurrections. I finished the book as I finished the essay, drawn to the parallels between this story and ours, and I remain glad to be a witch who does my best to cast counterspells against the binding hexes of apocalypse.

+ + +

The first system I understood was the biorhythm of the garden; then came the miracle of the alphabet. Third was the movement of the solar system. Even as a very young child, I was fascinated by representations of the heavens; my first word was "moon," and at four years old I remember describing a snippet of a past life involving leaning over a Renaissance-era telescope and seeing some cold blue orb blazing in the glass, but as soon as I spoke the memory aloud it was gone. I learned then to be careful speaking of other lives.

These systems engaged behaviors that I had not yet learned to name at all. It would be years before I recognized the oddity of some of my behaviors, and years after that that I would come to know that I might call them aspects of Autism and/or Obsessive Compulsive Disorder and/or neurodiversity and/or ritualist intuition. Whatever its name, what manifested is an obsession with the measurement of things: tracking the moon's phases and illumination levels, observing solstices and equinoxes, understanding irregular orbits, predicting eclipses, making charts labeling the stars I could see with my own eyes.

My mother, a naturalist and witch in her own right, offered me my first initiation into a nondenominational animist earth-based spiritual practice focused on observing the cycles of the living world. Instead of Christmas, we observed the Winter Solstice by candlelight as my mother explained why our hemisphere was at its darkest, using an orange as a model Earth, circling around a beeswax candle that represented our sun. My father, a mixed

Indigenous person who preferred time alone in the woods to most other activities, kept time similarly, by observation of nature, and thus I learned to tell time this way too; when the first camas blooms, last frost, early darkness, when you can hear the geese migrating overhead flying north, heavy dew on the snapdragons, when the strawberries ripen. I marked time, too, with the visibility of certain stars and the visitations or absences of the planets.

I was raised in relative social isolation on stolen Kalapuya territory in the so-called Willamette Valley. There amidst vine maple and skunk cabbage and ash and oak, among grapevines and apple orchards and hedges of sun warmed blackberries, I was unschooled by anarchist parents, no television or radio and minimal socializing, and there were many impulses I was encouraged to follow that other children are denied within typical overculture. I was allowed, for example, to awaken in the middle of the night and go out walking alone in the glittering frost-humped grazing fields under a high full moon in January, as long as I bundled up properly. I was six.

At a certain point my parents recognized my mystic impulses. Though they are both solitary practitioners of their own ancient and nameless ways, they recognized and mostly tolerated my need for teachers within intact traditions, my curiosity about churches and temples and psalms and prayer-forms. I began apprenticing with spirit people within a variety of traditions by the age of nine. I learned Tarot and astrology alongside an ever-deepening understanding of the biorhythms of the rural acreage we tended, a broadening vocabulary of incantations both sacred and mundane, and a more comprehensive knowledge of celestial mechanisms.

I was taught to feel witchcraft in my body, in the emergent neo-Pagan Goddess traditions of the West Coast in the 80s and 90s (ecstatic, feminist, sapphic lineages especially Starhawk, Ffiona Morgan, Judy Grahn, et al). In my training with the Order of Morgan and the Covenant of Hekate, I learned to heed sensations of hunger, pain, delight, tension, delirium, release, or virtually any other bodily impulse as holy tools at my disposal. I memorized Doreen Valiente's "Charge of the Goddess" and would sometimes repeat to myself:

Let my worship be within the heart that rejoiceth, for behold: all acts of love and pleasure are my rituals. And therefore let there be beauty and strength, power and compassion, honour and humility, mirth and reverence within you.

Altering the body's state in service of magic (going without food, or sweating in a pine bough ceremony, or imbibing psychotropics, or hanging in suspension, or dancing all night) was oftentimes an aspect of practice; a willful sacrifice in service of the heavenly mothers of old, a way of summoning our attentions to the present moment and to what was alive within us. What we were taught was essentially to slip between time in liminal states, to affect or witness the future or the past, by settling ourselves profoundly within the present.

I was not typically invited to participate in the most extreme gestures of dedication, as I was too young and novice, but I documented the devotion of my sisters watchfully, counting hours and steps, anticipating the advent of my own initiatory rites. I wondered where or when I would travel to, what I would witness, how I would be called upon to express my oracular gifts. I recognized that all of our ritualized somatic explorations seemed to alter time, by showing us different ways to count it.

The first time I kept watch over a ritual all night and witnessed the coming of the dawn, it felt like an eternity gone by: as I stumbled off toward well-earned sleep, my teachers reminded me with the rising sun: "Your body is your only possession; your attention is your only tool."

+ + +

I was raised also in an era of body-based public eco-ritual. I witnessed Julia Butterfly Hill's ascent into an ancient redwood, Ana Mendieta's *Siluetas* that looked so much like the chalk outline around her body after plummeting from her own apartment window during a fight with her partner Carl Andre, Yoko Ono's public grief rituals, Starhawk's public earth-healings. I saw my own teachers wail and beat their breasts in clearcuts, paint murals depicting the casualties of pollution, perform dance cycles about extinction. Together we protested animal testing, chained ourselves to logging gates, hung banners from bridges, occupied trees in danger of being killed.

It is very difficult to say when, precisely, I became sick. Chronic lung infections began at an early age; I would be diagnosed with asthma at nine. I was poisoned by swallowing cherry pits at three; the resulting cyanide poisoning from the partially-digested pits led to me having a seizure and being admitted to the hospital where, among other tests, I was given a spinal tap. I was not particularly hardy as a child; every flu or cold seemed to swoop down upon me without mercy. Throughout childhood I was enmired in troubles in my house of origin and suffered various traumas and abuses; I have an Adverse Childhood Experiences (ACE) score of 9. My body's long-term reactions to these travails would eventually be handily named C-PTSD and Obsessive Compulsive Disorder, diagnosed in 2019. I would also be diagnosed with Myalgic Encephalomyelitis/Chronic Fatigue Syndrome (ME/CFS) in 2020, and with severe endometriosis in 2022, after decades of suspecting one, the other, or both.

I was taught that all bodily impulses can be understood as a connection to godhead, and that changing our bodies deepens the ritual state. Yet somehow still when our bodies change with age or decrepitude or illness or grief or all of these, when bodies are touched by The Fates, this transformation is often not seen in our overculture, nor indeed within the majority of covens and witchy subculture, as service to the goddess. Whilst also seeking to dismiss all ableist tropes of the noble cripple, I do wonder: is not our own body still, always, the site of our worship? And therefore is not the observation of this distortion of time created by chronic ill health worth observing, as a place of wisdom, a site of suffering in exchange for holy knowledge, an embodied witness to the earth's agonies?

When bodies deteriorate into illness we are forced to keep time in a new and different way. It is said that the body cannot accurately remember pain; what does this mean for people who suffer from chronic, constant pain? How can I tell if this is any worse than usual? I (and many, many, many other chronically ill individuals) are forever on the razor's edge of not knowing if this is any worse than we usually expect. We measure heart rates, blood oxygenation levels, blood sugar, brain waves, vitamin B levels, weight, bowel movements, and anything else that's trackable. Our rituals are thus subverted, contained within a narrow way of tracking time.

When I started to become sick, I started to lose my faith. The traditions I was raised within denied me agency by lying and saying that my health was in my own hands. I absorbed ideas about blocked chakras and miasma theory, all the while my illness reduplicated. I believed I was cursed because of the pain I was constantly in. A past life must have seen me having back alley abortions, or killing my own children. Always a weak constitution, worsened by prolonged exposure to trauma, mold, and recurring infections in my lungs, kidneys, and bladder: the purifying organs, sickened within me.

I had heard of endometriosis but didn't have an accurate description of the disease, in spite of having studied herbal medicine, in spite of having had a midwife for a mother and a third wave feminist awakening. My impression before being diagnosed was that it was strictly a menstrual complaint, somehow related to estrogen levels, resulting in bad cramps and migraines. What I did not know (and that medical professionals are only just beginning to understand) is that endometriosis is a little-understood genetic condition that can affect people of any sex, including those who do not menstruate.

I have been deeply invested in the past several years in researching endometriosis as an epigenetic expression of sexual trauma, as persons with endometriosis are far likelier to have been victims of sexual abuse than persons without. I am beginning to understand, with horrible clarity, that epigenetics is real and tangible, that strange magicks do move upon the body in immeasurable ways.

The ableist argument that suggests that I or any other person with chronic ailments have the power to overcome my disability or illness through sheer will is incorrect and patronizing. We are as affected by our environments as our environments are upon us. Our bodies reflect the suffering our spirits have borne. Our traditions have taught us that gross matter, the physical body of both self and earth, is the place to which we must anchor ourselves in service of bending time, changing fate. Having a body is a temporary but deeply challenging assignment.

Perhaps, for sick witches, our illnesses are an aspect of our craft.

Perhaps some part of being a witch is serving as a canary in a coalmine: sensing the poison early, heeding the call for remediation.

+ + +

Where we get the word "witch" is somewhat uncertain.

We can trace it to the Old English: *wicce,* "female magician, sorceress," in later use especially "a woman supposed to have dealings with the devil or evil spirits and to be able by their cooperation to perform supernatural acts," fem. of Old English *wicca,* "sorcerer, wizard, man who practices witchcraft or magic," from verb *wiccian,* "to practice witchcraft" (compare Low German *wikken, wicken,* "to use witchcraft," *wikker, wicker,* "soothsayer").

In his seminal anthropological text *The White Goddess,* Robert Graves, in discussing the willow which is sacred to Hekate, connects the word to a root *wei- which connotes bending or pliance, by saying: "Its connection with witches is so strong in Northern Europe, that the words 'witch' and 'wicked' are derived from the same ancient word for willow, which also yields 'wicker'." Not all linguists agree, but nonetheless I was taught some version of this: that the word witch was associated with the capacity to bend, to warp and to weave, as one might make a basket.

We have no means of understanding precisely how our distant ancestors experienced time, but we can tell that there were strong associations between the idea of fate and the various practices of weaving, whether by hand or by loom, baskets or carpets or tapestries. These crafts were strongly associated with witches and seers.

Perhaps because performing one's craft can access flow state in which time seems to move differently, association with time's measurement and witchcraft is also immortal. In most ancient cultures, there seem to have been multiple described states of time: chaos and kairos in Greek, for example, an ordered time and a disordered one. We find glimmers of this connection in the stories of the Fates, the Norn, Demeter (who gives us our words for various forms of "meting"—"meter" being one of these). Think of the tale of Sleeping Beauty, of the spindle (a symbol of the weaver) that is enchanted to warp time forcing everyone in the castle to sleep for 100 years. Think of the Horae, sacred temple dancers who kept time in the ancient world according to the celestial clocks and planetary hours (see also the hora, the traditional Jewish dance), whose name would give way to our word "whore" but also, in Spanish, *hora* or hour. All these ways we passed The Time.

Thus, to call oneself a witch was originally, perhaps, a metaphoric or poetic representation of our etheric labors, a way to announce one's place as a weaver of time.

We also have come to discuss such things as "deep time," in relationship with knowledge of the living earth and its holy cycles. One impulse that seems apparent amongst all witches, whether people of that description are initiates of an ancient order or are a self-taught TikTok warlock, is this innate urge to seek out ways to stretch and expand our perception of time. As a witchbaby (shoutout to Francesca Lia Block forever), I would practice my own little offerings of my own form: holding my breath underwater for as long as I could while slow-chanting the name of my patron goddess in my mind, meting out my breath with a stopwatch I had borrowed. How quickly could I move across a mile? How slowly? Could I count every rose on my way home? Always, I was thinking about the old soothsaying rhyme about seeing a certain number of crows, always I was noticing patterns in phone numbers.

Now I most often interpret my OCD as an impulse toward ritual, toward aligning things and surrendering to a real, if rigid, type of beauty. I indulge my pattern-finding capacity as a professional astrologer, in my own daily observations of the planetary hours, and in the tending of my altars.

The planetary hours, based on the Chaldean order (slowest- to fastest-moving as the planets appear in the sky) are an ancient system in which one of the seven classical planets is given rulership over each day and various parts of the day, beginning with the hour of dawn. The classical planets are those visible to us. In Chaldean order, they are Saturn, Jupiter, Mars, the Sun,

A CONFLUENCE OF WITCHES

Venus, Mercury, and the Moon, and they take rulership over the hours in this sequence. This way of keeping time is the origin of the names of the days of the week as used in English and most other European languages, and it is oft-utilized in a variety of heritage magick traditions (i.e. crafting Mars charms at dawn on a Tuesday, for example).

For years now, I have been striving to align my days as much as I am able with the planetary hours. I frequently make decisions about things as arbitrary as responding to an email or watering my plants in alignment with the planetary hours: Wednesdays are big email and writing days for me; on Sundays at dawn I intone hymns and water my houseplants, attending to them, listening. I am aware that I am creating my own time-rhythms that differ from those of the larger world; as silly as it sounds it feels somehow important, knowing how many of us are doing just this.

+ + +

As a child, driving between our farmhouse and town, I would see a piece of graffiti under an overpass, a blue and green orb with the word OZONE? put up next to it. I was terrified of the hole in the ozone layer. Terrified of a megaquake, a volcano, a tidal wave, something uncontrollable and godsent. My parents had read *Silent Spring* and Wendell Berry and were at times almost Luddites; they were not optimistic about the future, and they raised me within their doubt. I remember marking new clearcuts on the way to my mentor's cabin, crying there in a fresh lumber scar after my first love suicided. I remember when I was fleeing white nationalists, driving with my best friend through the charred ruins of my childhood fishing spots, the river running black with ash. Getting used to orange skies, air quality literally off the charts bad. Tending smokesick songbirds in my bathroom, with air purifiers and jar lids full of clean water, my cats too lethargic to even chase them. Watching my friends die of rare cancers, of bad drugs that distort their departing spirits, of despair by their own hands.

I am listening to requiems while watching the smoke on the horizon, staring at the algae choking the creek. I am bringing buckets of water to the parched deer and watching the does whose necks are crawling with ticks as they slurp gratefully from the buckets I do not really have the strength to carry. I am doing what I can, moving cactus pups and planting native milkweed, counting the butterflies who drift elegantly past on tattered wings. I am witnessing the sadness of the stonefruit trees rendered barren by frost, and that of my chickens laying early, frantic with the hormonal panic-messages of the living world. Early puberty, bleeding sick. Messengers from the Underworld, come to warn us.

And yet: for as long as there have been records of human writ, there have been foretellings of annihilation and doom. The fear of death has never been far from our heels, and there are so many ways to destroy a world: meteor strike, plague, rapid heating, rapid cooling, exploitation, colonization, war, pestilence, smogbanks over Los Angeles. Overdoses, accidents, murders.

Practicing astrology is comforting to me; the planets move in their predictable little arcs, the stars so rarely flicker or fail and when they do it brings us miracles. So we wait for Betelgeuse to supernova, anticipating the beauty of the heavenly event. I measure and measure and compare and make stories of the ineffable.

+ + +

In 1947, a group of nuclear scientists who had worked on the Manhattan Project came together to create a metaphorical representation of humanity's proximity to annihilating danger. After the atomic bombings of Hiroshima and Nagasaki, they, in what can arguably be seen as a state of profound remorse, began publishing a mimeographed newsletter, *Bulletin of the Atomic Scientists,* which, since its inception, has depicted the Doomsday Clock on every cover. The artist who designed the Clock, Langsdorf, chose a clock to reflect the urgency of the problem: like a countdown, the Doomsday Clock suggests that destruction will naturally occur unless someone takes action to stop it.

It was initially set at seven minutes to midnight, with midnight representing doom for all of humanity.

On January 24, 2023, accounting for such threats as nuclear escalation, climate change, COVID-19, and risks associated with disinformation, the Clock was moved to ninety seconds before midnight, meaning that the Clock's current setting is the closest it has ever been to midnight since its inception.

When a witch becomes ill, a Doomsday Clock is planted within their bodily workings, a knowledge of the inevitable. We encounter our mortality abruptly, repeatedly, arduously, as the ground gives way beneath us and we are swallowed up by the aching earth. A whole new glossary of feeling emerges. The body becomes a crone before the spirit is prepared. Time collapses.

channeled writing excerpt, 1/23/23:

time distorts. all is dreamlike. i have awakened and my head is pounding, eyes jiggling with each thrum of my swollen brainstem. i know my pulse rate because of the fitbit i have wearily accepted that i must wear: the endometriosis colonizing my chest cavity demands that i monitor my blood oxygenation levels. so i know that my pulse rate is 92 bpm, blood oxygenation at 92%. somehow, the distance between floods of blood becomes eternal. it is my quieting breath, my calling my blood back into peace. cutting through ptsd with my athame, righting time.

i want to be a million places at once. dear gods, grant me clemency, let me drift amidst the worlds. i don't know who else to ask. let me be somewhere else.

+ + +

A skilled witch is capable of being in two times at once.

It is said that very powerful witches can be in two places at once, but that flickers along the edges of credibility for most of us, living as we do in this leaden age of dogmatic materialism. Mostly though, we might agree that mysticism in general is the capacity to cultivate a wholehearted presence while also exploring something unpresent—witchcraft in specific may be understood to be this dual perspective and the added layer of working to bend some aspect of that perception. This is a balancing act! The danger of investing too much attention in these unseen realms is not to be understated: many people have been institutionalized, shunned, abused, and killed for announcing what is beheld in the unseen, or they have ventured into intellectual danger that arises when one completely departs from consensus reality. And simultaneously, we can argue that all art comes from this particularly human ability to imagine.

Witchcraft, I was always taught, is all about honing the imagination, focusing the mind. The tools and the memorized chants and the symbols and the aesthetics may be helpful or evocative, but they are not the craft itself. The craft itself is that bending, weaving, imagining, while also staying anchored.

When witches reach forward in time in our attempts to prevent or repair harm, when we reach across ancestral chasms to mend and remediate the past, we are holding two states at once: the present and the nonpresent. It is our labor that is braiding them together; our labor which creates the world.

When engaged in our craft, there is something that moves us into the future, envisioning a path, enabling us to move forward.

With all of the interest of late in mycelial networks, dark matter, artificial intelligence and machine learning, connective tissue, spiderwebs, one would expect that we might soon come to accept that the reality we live within is defined by a multitude of signals—the imaginations of many, many, many beings. The idea here is that perhaps the practices of symbolic thinking and ritual (also understood as witchcraft) are forever linking us to one another, creating a network of thought that defines and orders the universe. It is not our responsibility to change our fate, but it is our responsibility to fully feel our way through it, to process our aliveness.

It is not so much that our craft can alter the actuality of things, but more that ritualistic meaning-making can alter the way we experience them. For the last year or so, I have been deeply investigating the colour pink. I was intrigued most of all because pink is an imaginary colour: red and ultraviolet are the two ends of the visible spectrum, and yet our minds insist on constructing a colour that cannot be measured by science. I don't know quite how I can convey the importance of this to myself and witches everywhere. What I mean is: we have no way to understand pink but as "pink"—thus, our perception of something does alter our way of being with it. We experience something as real, predictable, normal, which is in fact inexplicable and full of mystery.

What else, one wonders, might we be experiencing within the imaginal only? In what other ways can our minds create things outside the realm of measure? Can we imagine entirely new worlds, or new ways of walking within them? Could we already be existing in entirely new worlds?

+ + +

I consider the question of whether I could survive unmedicated in a functional indigenous community to be a moot point, though this is a point sometimes raised against the disability justice movement as a question by cryptofascist spiritual movements. Primitivism makes no exception for wheelchairs, etc.

As many incredible scholars of disability justice have taught us, and particularly in the words of Leah Lakshmi Peipzna-Samarasinha: "The future is disabled." There are increasing incidents of autoimmune illness, autism, neurodiversity, post-viral conditions, inflammatory conditions, allergies, connective tissue disorders—and whether they are environmentally triggered or newly properly diagnosed, the end result is the same: more and more of us are being summoned into new time rhythms by virtue of falling ill. Are we then, as disabled witches, being asked to keep time with the earth? Are we being asked to embody and transform some subtle energy that animates all things?

Perhaps by pacing the breath, by observing our dreams, by heeding our limits, by being with ourselves in suffering, perhaps we are conjuring a worldly witness that will change the arc of time. We practice even when we do not have the strength, even when the way ahead looks dim. We are relieved when the rains come, ever relieved when the rains come.

A guiding question for us in this time may be:

If my traditions teach me that my body is one with the earth, and the earth has been and continues to be brutalized, and so has my body, how can

I make my material existence a site of healing for both my body and for the earth?

. . . .

Body As Ecosystem Meditation

This exercise is similar to a body scan. The intention is to view ecological remediation as an action within the body, and vice versa, so as to see what healing we might accomplish when we remember ourselves as one with the earth. It can be undertaken anywhere and can last any amount of time you like, but I prefer to set aside twenty minutes or so and be in a quiet and comfortable place with minimal distraction—over time, as with all visualizations, it may become easier and more efficient to drop into. The intention is to view ecological remediation as an action within the body, and vice versa, so as to see what healing we might accomplish when we remember ourselves as one with the earth.

Exercise:

Let's imagine, then, our body as an ecosystem. Eventually your body can express multiple biomes at once, have multiple needs, but let's start simply. Think of a few climates or environments (desert, savannah, alpine meadow, tundra, deciduous forest, marsh. . .) and allow yourself to investigate which of these your body feels in alignment with.

As you begin with awareness at your toes and the soles of your feet, ask yourself questions:

Is this part of your body cold? Hot? Dry? Damp? Stiff? Limpid? Tense? Lax? Which climates can you connect with, which landscape can you see yourself as?

Where do these sensations bring you? Stiff joints may feel like melting icebergs, or perhaps our tension headaches are like droughts. In acute illness, we may shudder and sweat like a hurricane or groan and split in agony like an earthquake.

As with a body scan, where we might observe discomfort and send attention there, here we might visualize our bodily discomfort as an aspect of ecological calamity and envision the ecological repair that might alleviate suffering: if we are feeling expansive and unstable with swift breath, and we have aligned with an alpine environment, we may visualize our anxiety around stillness as quaking aspens exuding excess pollen in response to drought. We may visualize a soft and calm wind settling, gentling, the air cooling, moisture condensing and dewing upon us, heat expunged. If we have found ourselves akin to a burning conifer forest, we might call rain down upon us, which may appear as a cleansing flood of tears. Perhaps we feel deeply frozen, strip-mined, clearcut.

Can we invite ourselves to thaw, to repair, to regrow?

Can we see our scars stitched with flowers, our aches warmed by life-giving sun?

. . . .

By acknowledging the imbalances, the places of disease and injury, and by visualizing them as sites of repair, is one sure way to be in intimacy with the earth.

El Regreso (The Return)

BY MADRE JAGUAR

It hasn't been that long

Since Children of Earth forgot,
Our unique place in ALL of Creation
The medicine of the web and the mycelium
Everything and everyone
Interconnected in symbiotic relation

It hasn't been that long

We are made in the image of the Mother
This was common knowledge
We understood her seasons and cycles,
The ebb and flow, time to create, time to birth, time to rest,
Time in between to deconstruct and reassess

It hasn't been that long

Only 500 years in Turtle Island
Compared to millions of years before
We were in tune and in sync
With moon and stars, sun, clouds and sky

Minerals, plants, and animals
Together, dancing the eternal dance

It hasn't been that long

Since we strayed from the path of beauty
Our minds clouded with doubt and discontent
True purpose forgotten: to be in sacred service
As pollinators, gardeners, dreamers, creators.
Not hunters. Not destroyers. Lovers!

It hasn't been that long, our siblings, the trees
still remember and some of them witnessed it first hand
when you ask them, they will tell you
in their quiet wisdom, with love and grief
in their roots and their hearts
"We were in right relationship once"

It hasn't been that long

The mountains and the stones will tell you
You are abundant by Nature
This is ancestral wisdom as old as the world
There is enough, plenty for each of us to thrive
Lack and distrust only means you forgot

It hasn't been that long

Water remembers it well,

Each drop encoded with memory

We knew her to be Sacred, the blue print for ALL Life

We sang our prayers and we blessed her

Full of gratitude we called her Mother

And our internal waters resonate with this knowledge

It hasn't been that long

And if you ask Grandfather Fire

He will crackle in delight

Telling stories of those who came before

Who sat in council and prayed for guidance

Shared stories and songs, only a few generations ago

It hasn't been that long

Remember, we are the bridges and the portals

Our own hearts, the center point

Between Heaven and Earth,

East, South, West and North

In perfect harmony and perfect balance, between the worlds

It hasn't been that long

Yet there is no time to waste, it can no longer be ignored
As long as there is breath in our lungs, there is work to be done
Divine Union means remembering, reconnecting
Returning to the roots and reweaving the threads
We are One Nature, One Organism, One people
We are Love made visible.

Return, return, return . . . it hasn't been that long.

CHAPTER 7

COVEN-WORK

*How to Organize, Gather,
and Evolve Together*

COVEN WORK IS AN ENACTMENT of and a participation in the web of relations which we are all inextricably a part of. Whether you are a solitary witch, a community leader, a coven member, or a friend, your witchcraft is relational. Your coven can be the cosmos. Modern witches have a specific responsibility to be aware of the communal nature of existence. Through that awareness, one realizes that all the spells we cast ripple through and affect all the worlds.

The magic of modern witchcraft is communal. Because we are aware of the symbiotic relationships we exist within, our magic is radically attuned to big spells for collective wellbeing. Each of us plays an integral role in building a new world rooted in reciprocity and respect for each other and the planet. Modern witchcraft by its very nature insists on practices and approaches that send impactful ripples out into the wider realm of community and collective. Craft your personal love spells so that they are also love spells for the land, for the city, for all people. There are no small spells.

A central organizing principle for modern witchcraft is acknowledging the effects of all of our practices on both local and cosmic scales. In order for our witchcraft to be revolutionary it must be reflexive and transpersonal, healing for ourselves and for all those we commune with, in this realm and beyond. There are nuanced concerns and ways to approach this work for both the solo worker, and for communities of witches—with varying degrees of complexity for each way of organizing self and others. When thinking about ways to organize or structure one's practice, let it be in the highest harmonic good for whom it affects.

As an organization, Modern Witches has always strived to create spaces that feel welcoming to a wide range of spirit workers, cultures, and identities. The work of being truly inclusive is an ongoing process of evaluation, reca- libration, and a conversation with complexity. Soft and strong boundaries, a willingness to listen, and a diverse circle of witches fostering restorative and liberatory relationships, are integral to cultivating welcoming spaces for witches to explore their magic. The commitment to diversity and inclusion within groups of witches is dependent upon an individual witch's commitment to justice and liberation work in their own lives and practices. A modern witch is actively learning their own history, and respecting the histories of others. Our own sense of responsibility and willingness to learn from others is key to creating healthy and healing communities where honoring multiple spiritual paths is possible.

At the heart of this work is a tender heart that desires friendship and mutual magical support. Whether you are looking for ways to convene your own coven of creatrixes, organizing for a cause, or simply looking to foster magical relationships, these reflections offer insights into how to be in community as carer, teacher, and friend.

—Casey

Herbalism as Mutual Aid

BY DAMIANA

Do you ever dream of the world you want to live in? Have you considered a world where everyone could live a dignified life? Have you dreamt collectively about this world? It is long overdue for us to take action for that dream to come true. Let's step into living that dream together.

Dreaming of this new world began for me with recognizing that the systems of oppression currently in place are vulnerating global majorities, leaving more and more individuals and communities unable to have their basic needs met. I've both observed this around me, and embodied it being born a woman of color, amongst other things. Mutual aid is a way of resisting this violence; it can look like many different things, but they all need a collective organization to take care of each other. We must remember we are not alone.

What is mutual aid and what can it look like? Long before having the language, many of us were raised in cultures where reciprocity and solidarity were an everyday normalized way to live. Recognizing herbalism as a political practice (from access to plants and knowledge, to time and resources, to craft, commodification, etc.) allows us to fight oppression at many levels, while supporting the healing of ourselves and our relations both at a physical and energetic level.

Herbalism is people's knowledge. Even though there are closed practices that must be respected as such, the act of creating relationships with plants and working with them in order to take care of ourselves and each other belongs to all the peoples. As I've prioritized my herbalism practice the last few years, anti-oppression work and specifically mutual aid have become a pillar for me. In order to really feel like it's a community exercise, I've focused on organizing and sharing knowledge, resources, and remedies.

I was born into a family and a culture where, even though there was no language for it, mutual aid was woven into the fabric of daily life. Countless examples of this type of care from my childhood glow in my memory and remain present. Folx feeding many blood and chosen family members, including elderly friends who would otherwise eat alone or not at all; practicing our reading skills by reading stories to younger children; getting together to paint someone's house; organizing ride shares and clothing swaps; offering support to someone struggling with addiction. . . No matter if it was unspoken, the spirit of support was always present.

None of these examples were special occasions; most of my family were not intentionally politicized, but I now see how in their own way they value occupying the spaces where they could resist systems of oppression. How they share resources beyond money, how they care about their communities having their needs met, how they know to give and receive in reciprocity, and how they're invested in cultivating meaningful relations, just because that's the way we do things. And by we, I mean so many of us. These were not things that I experienced on my own; many of my friends and acquaintances had similar experiences and can relate in their particular way.

I share here because this shaped me, it made me who I am. At my core I like to think of myself as a carer, someone who cares about others, who cares for others. I see my purpose in life as one of service and as such, I acknowledge mutual aid as my responsibility in practicing herbalism, in order for it to be a communal practice. Recognizing that our own liberation is intertwined with everyone's liberation.

We don't come from a place of saving anyone; we come from a place of listening and responding to what people ask for the best way we can. Sometimes it's big projects that require more resources, skills and capacity, like working with Indigenous authorities who want to have a traditional clinic serving everyone in town. We follow their lead and receive by learning from their/our old ways. We bring back knowledge that was stolen and remedies they don't have time to prepare; we get to sit in ceremony and we take in the wisdom and work on ourselves.

Other times it's small projects that only take a few minutes. Making an extra cup of calming herbal tea and offering it to our roommate/partner/coworker when we've heard they're stressed. We need to move away from the capitalist standards of productivity, because truly every little action counts. There is pleasure in the commitment of working toward our own healing and the healing of our communities, which are one and the same; this includes rest and taking breaks as needed. When we do this work collectively, we know that some will step up when others step back; we are all there for each other. We are in constant movement, expanding and contracting, accelerating and slowing down, giving and receiving.

The pandemic made it clear how fragile we are when we focus on our individuality, and how much impact we can have when we co-create to support each other. I'm a big fan of steam remedies; I was honored to share knowledge around how to make steams at home and sourcing antiviral and calming herbs accessible to many to take care of our respiratory and nervous systems. I also collaborated with many herbalists to support specific communities who reached out. For example, a friend of a friend was a nurse and in a casual conversation was sharing how she and her coworkers were so overwhelmed at the hospital. We organized and put together little pampering kits for them to find a moment to moisturize with infused oil, take a bath with herbal salts, and enjoy daily adaptogenic beverages. We were called in to care for the carers.

The needs are not always what they seem; we will learn how to act by nurturing our relations, by asking questions, listening and not making assumptions, by proposing and finding a path together with the folx who will be receiving. Their choices and wants should be centered, the same way ours should be when we are the ones asking for support. While a lot of the work we did during the pandemic was to support immunity through tinctures and syrups, half of my work during 2020 and 2021 was supporting people's nervous system and emotional health with herbs.

I am completely obsessed with flower essences because of their subtle energetic impact in our lives and the magic they invite into our days. They require a small investment in a little alcohol, jars, water, and labels. They preserve the medicine of a flower signature in a moment in time through the alchemy of light imprinting the electromagnetic field of a specific flower in water, which we can keep communing with by preserving that water and diluting it. They can be eternally diluted and the medicine just gets more and more subtle, meaning going deeper and deeper into our psyches. I always feel they want to be shared widely and I've made huge batches to offer and distribute in protests, camps, and other rebel actions.

I speak of herbalism because it's my main tool, but herbalism isn't the only need—any gift you have can be put to service. You don't have to be raised like some of us were raised; perhaps you learned about caring for community as an adult, perhaps you're only getting curious now. Every experience of community care is valid.

You don't need experience in order to show up for others or to ask for help from others. You just need to commit to offering care, and get together with others to work on a project. Remember that no one needs to be saved, and that you don't have to work outside of your own community. Under these systems of oppression we live in, I'm sure it won't be hard to find a need that's not being met. Perhaps someone would welcome a meal train right now, someone else is interested in learning a skill that you may have, or everyone would like to have a talking circle where you can hold space for each other to voice your mind and heart and be witnessed.

Cultivating radical tenderness in our relations with ourselves and others is important as we do this work. We will make mistakes, and other folx will make mistakes, no matter how long we've been organizing. It's important to resist punitive reactions and give and receive feedback in a compassionate way. It is okay to not know how. Find someone who can teach you some tools! Normalize being perfectly imperfect. Take a step toward offering care today.

We Measure the Sea:
A Declaration of Art as Magic as Connection

BY ELIZA SWANN AKA EMERALD

"This hope isn't something I've sought.
This silent wing of the Unknown University."—Roberto Bolano

The sun was heavy white, the trees were burdened low with dust—we were pressed flat by the roasting air as we labored up the steep slope of the mountain. The summer sky was such a hot dry blue there was no linear space; from every point of motion you collapsed back into a plane of heat and light that made it seem like you weren't moving forward at all. I was thirty-one and trudging through the ancient ruins of Delphi alone, surrounded by throngs of tourists.

Dating back to 1400 BCE, Delphi was the most important shrine in Greece and its oracles were the most famous in the Western world for their prophecy. Built around a sacred spring, Delphi was considered to be the *omphalos*, the navel of the world. People came from all over to have their questions about the future answered. The allure of Delphi—though a living oracle hasn't prophesied there in nearly a thousand years—still brings thousands of tourists each day crushing through the turnstiles to take photographs of the toppled pillars that remain.

This trip to Delphi was a final attempt to find a place in this world; I was looking for reasons to live. Some months earlier, I had finished graduate school at Central St Martins in London—a grueling experience of academic browbeating that took the imagination out of my head, the only thing I'd had to get me through a troubled adolescence and into adulthood. I grew up in New York City, where from my pre-teen years onward I had found family among a handful of teenage queer punks on the Lower East Side—most of us were witches. At sixteen, I dropped out of high school and enrolled in college painting classes while also taking initiations into Hermetic Orders. I studied alchemy, and tried to figure out what an "art world" is. How it came to pass that I was a teenage drop-out studying Hermeticism and painting at the same time is a long story. For now, I'll just say that there was a lucky combination of being left completely to my own devices, a latchkey kid with no one waiting for them at home, and I had an insatiable thirst for art. Somehow, I graduated with an art degree after several years of intermittent attendance at different art schools.

In the early aughts you had to keep your mysticism secret if you wanted to be thought of as sane or intelligent—in most life circumstances this is still true. I made paintings about priestesses, prophets, and alchemy, but when galleries visited I spoke about these subjects as "research." I spoke about the size and color of a painting, as if I were describing the make and model of a car, instead of describing the curved lines of my own spirit. It wasn't that I cared whether these art people thought I was an airhead. I just wanted to sell some paintings and pay the rent, so I spoke about accepted topics.

In my twenties I scraped together a living working as a florist and a psychic-for-hire. I was training in the esoteric arts, and having difficulty convincing my teachers to bend the Renaissance-era magical techniques they were teaching into our own time and language. I wanted them to be unafraid of change, to stop being homophobic and racist, to listen to some experimental music with me. They wouldn't. I wasn't showing much art, so I opened a little storefront gallery with my partner at the time so we could hang our friends' art somewhere visible. I wanted all the people I loved to be *seen*.

One afternoon in my twenty-ninth year, I gave a woman a Tarot reading in the storefront—that was how I covered the $500 rent. She had just come back from studying at Central St Martins and she encouraged me to apply, assuring me they'd love my work. Without much preparation, I applied. I got in two weeks later, and began to prepare to move to England in a few months' time. Suddenly I was desperate to *teach*! With a master's degree I could do that! I would find a way to blend the mystical with the visual—after all, magic is an *art*—I would teach that in colleges. And why not? I had a vision and so it must be true. That was how I lived my life then.

I thought nothing about taking out enormous student loans or leaving my partner and the home and gallery we built behind—I just followed the scent. It made sense for me to go to England. The Swanns had come from there, and though their legacy was an unhappy one, I held out hope that my return would bring a sense of belonging that I hadn't found anywhere else. Family legend held that Albert Swann, my great-great grandfather, murdered someone in a bar fight and smuggled himself onto a boat to Philadelphia to avoid the hangman's noose. My aunt who was a witch changed her last name to Swann just before she died, cutting the men in her life loose from her story and taking her mother's maiden name. I took that last name too, shortly after her death when I was fifteen.

Albert Swann and I both had a terrible time of it in London. Though it fulfilled a lifelong dream for me to be able to walk alone to the Tate Britain to sit with William Blake's art, nothing else seemed to come together. I had a job in a flower shop that lasted one week before they fired me. This happened two more times. I took out more loans, ate rolls of biscuits for most meals, and slept in a cramped room in a council flat with too many roommates. I hitched rides to sacred sites to visit megaliths and monoliths. I was cold and lost a lot. My partner and I fell apart in slow motion while I was away—he wanted me home. I never thought I could find one, and didn't recognize our apartment in New York as a place of safety, though it was.

What made me unhappy wasn't that I was having a rough time getting by, I'd experienced that before. It was the *school* I went to. They confined the fine artists into a damp old building that was falling apart. I was assigned a tutor whose role was to support my development as an artist during my time at school. At our first meeting, she surveyed me with her ice blue eyes and said I had no business visiting the megalithic sites I told her I was excited to see. I wasn't from England, I wouldn't understand them. In subsequent meetings, she let me know that all psychics are frauds, that my work possessed no intellectual rigor, and that one of my major shortcomings was that I talked too much. We spent a lot of time sitting in a prickly kind of silence.

Group critiques went much the same way. We'd all just shuffle our feet on the sopping wet studio carpet and say as little as possible. The only students who seemed to get any funding or positive feedback were two very tall and manly men who made very large sculptures. Though not at all uncommon in the art world, I thought this place would be different. I thought I would come find community, and discover in their art and words more facets in this jewel of a world.

The only people who cheered for my art at the institution were two technicians who worked in the video department. They were horror movie fans who liked the "witchy shite" I was making. For the commencement show, I made an installation for them. I put a crooked old play-house together that I painted black on the outside and neon green on the inside. When you walked in, a video was playing of me sticking my head into a hole I'd dug in the sand behind Derek Jarman's house, while the sound of witches describing their initiations into witchcraft played in the background. They loved it—no one else said much.

At the end of two years, I couldn't figure out what art was or why a person would care. I'd been silenced and told my interests had no place in the "real" art world. Nevermind that scholars and art world elite came to me for Tarot readings on the sly to help them solve creative problems. I'd left home, borrowed more money than I could ever hope to repay to get to England, and now that I had to leave I had nowhere to go and nothing to do when I got there. The world was bent under gray glass, all sounds muted. It was summer, if you could call it that—the air churned out a constant gray flood of mist that crept into every warm place to chill it— and my visa was expiring in a month.

Many people have written about breakdowns and depression, but do any of us do it well? It had been too many years of being told my faiths were not real and not relevant. Art and language left me for the first time, and left nothing in its place. My head was empty. Later I would learn to treasure nothingness as the true face of the divine—but I am getting ahead of myself. At that point I felt desperate and unfocused, unable to hear the living world, and deeply unnerved by the silence.

Eventually, a credit card offer arrived, sent to me in a big bundle of letters that had gone to my old New York address. I'd go to Delphi, I decided. I'd ask the place of the oracles what to do. I activated the credit card and booked my trip for the following week. I can't tell you *why* that was the only thing to do, but it was. I threw a few things in a backpack and left without much of a plan except that I'd go to where the oracles at Delphi had sat and ask their bones for help.

Originally, Delphi was dedicated to the Earth goddess Gaia who was guarded by a serpent called Pytho. According to legends, Apollo killed Pytho and forced Gaia to leave Delphi and the oracle was kept in her place but was now annointed as the mouthpiece of the sky god Apollo—the oracle was then named Pythia after the slain snake.

The last recorded Oracle to give prophecy at Delphi was in 393 CE, when by order of the Christian Emperor Theodosius I, the temple was closed and never reopened. Between 389 and 391 he issued the "Theodosian decrees" which established a ban on Paganism—temples were ransacked and burned, the remaining Pagan holidays that had not yet been rendered Christian were abolished, and auspices and magic were deemed punishable offenses. There was now one God: he was a man, and he dwelt indoors in a church. Delphi fell into ruin until 1892, when a team of French archaeologists directed by Théophile Homolle of the Collège de France excavated the site.

Victorian historians claimed that the Pythia delivered prophecy in a frenzied state induced by vapors rising from a chasm in the ground, and that she spoke gibberish that male priests turned into intelligible poems, later preserved in Greek literature. This idea has been challenged by modern scholars who argue that ancient sources uniformly represent the Pythia speaking intelligibly, giving prophecies in her own voice. Herodotus, for example, describes the Pythia speaking clearly in dactylic hexameters.

Looking back on it now, the silencing of the oracles led directly to my own story of being told that my words were gibberish before being silenced altogether at art school. Academia's complete dismissal of intuition and direct transmission as viable sources of information stem from the Roman Empire's Emperor Theodosius I silencing all worship save that of the city-dwelling sky god who spoke only to priests. The stage had already been set by the patriarchal Greek culture that celebrated taking the Earth goddess out of the oracles' mouth and replacing their voices with that of the sky god. Colonial culture continues to skew its measure of intelligence and comfort toward the "rational male" who dwells in cities and to model its definition of stupidity and terror after an "irrational female" who dwells in nature. Although we now know these ideas are poisonous constructs in academia, their effect feels permanent. We'll have to level these schools and start again; I have dedicated my life to this thought.

None of that history was on my mind as I left London for Greece that June. I can't recall how I got there exactly. I vaguely recall crashing in a hostel before getting to Delphi on a bus jammed with tourists who tried to make small talk. Then I was on a path on a day so hot the sky wiped out the stones. Eventually, I walked over to the small pile of pillars that were left where the oracle used to sit, just past the treasury where gifts for her would have been left. I hadn't brought these dead women any offerings; my grief had turned me too inward. I hadn't planned any great speech, either. I stood there suddenly ashamed—all my internal organs exposed so that the slightest breeze made me wince—that I had come to ask the spirits of the oracles for help empty handed.

I was pushed or I fell, I'm not sure which, onto my hands and knees like a dog. I bent my face low and spit on the earth—this was a precious gift in this heat. My knee was bleeding a little and I offered this too.

I whispered the question that had brought me there and didn't elaborate: "Oracle—what do I *do*?" and without a pause I heard:

"GO HOME. GO BACK TO NEW YORK. TEACH ART AND MAGIC AS ONE DISCIPLINE. GO!" I waited a while for more and heard "GO!" one more time—it sounded irritable.

I stood up and brushed the dust off, not bothering to explore the rest of the site. I waited for the bus, a horse with blinders—I had one thing to do—GO.

Simone Weil says in her book *Waiting for God* that "Creative attention means really giving our attention to what does not exist." And that is what I did from that day to this—if there was no school where magic and art could be taught together, I would make one. I went back to New York and began teaching classes about Tarot, scrying, and divination. I looked for ways to teach esoteric topics to artists. I lived with friends, owned little, remained poised, and waited for further instruction.

Based on my own experience, magic is a force akin to gravity or light—it is essential, inherent, sentient—existing for its own purposes and by its own rules. We can bend magic so it produces and amplifies particular results, just as we can bend white light through a prism to produce refractions of color. This is where art comes in. We bend the forces of magic through ritual, sound, image, and poetry to point its energy in a particular direction to produce an astounding array of quantum outcomes. This is the basis of my teachings, and from that time to this, I have taught various techniques for using art to wield magic.

When the inspiration struck about a year later I decided to start an art school for mystics. It was a fool's errand, but one that persists. I had no financial or institutional backing, no business acumen, no administrative skills. I still don't. I asked a raven I saw in a tree if I should go ahead with the idea and they said, "Yes—now—call it the Golden Dome." Though that sounds annoyingly like the Golden Dawn with whom I am not affiliated, I asked no questions. I took the bird's words down as dictation, or at least what I thought they were. I had nothing to lose at that time—that was a great gift that Central St Martins gave me. Nothing. A short time later I was at a dinner party filled with art world people when the host silenced the table and asked me to tell everyone about my school idea. I started to speak about magic and art when he abruptly interrupted me: "Who's going to attend? Who's going to want to learn from *you?* What credentials do you have?" Words flew out of my mouth like steam gushing out of a crack in the earth—"I'm nobody. That's why this'll work." I was no one with nothing—how could I fail?

In many respects I am an adherent to negative theology which posits that no finite knowledge can fully know the infinite, so that we can only seek to know by accessing that which is beyond and above knowledge, what Pseudo-Dionysius, an enigmatic 6th century negative theologian, calls the "Divine Darkness." In his work *Mystical Theology* he asks us to "pray that we may come unto this Darkness which is beyond light, and, without seeing and without knowing, to see and to know that which is above vision and knowledge through the realization that by not-seeing and by unknowing we attain to true vision and knowledge." The paradox here is that many of us who recognize the failings of language become poets, those of us that see the inadequacy of representation become artists, those of us that understand the limitations of thought become philosophers, those of us who see schools falling short teach and so on. It was in this spirit that I was glad to be nobody starting a school with nothing. Where else is there to begin?

The Golden Dome has gone on to produce artist residencies, exhibitions, and classes for the past ten years, since 2014. In the fiber of its existence is an argument for a school that can encompass both faith and reason, intuition and rational deduction, gut instinct and empirical science. Jeffrey Kripal in his work *The Serpent's Gift* describes his ideal learning space as a "third classroom," a space in which a student can use a method that "combines faithful and rationalist re-readings even as it moves beyond both." The subject-object split of the Western Enlightenment which still dominates intellectual discourse has hurt us; you can not be a "self" observing a separate "world," there is no true separation. What the Golden Dome can do, if nothing else, is connect things.

In the early days of the school, I rented a house out in the California desert to hold an artist residency. Sarah Johnson came and taught a class where we were instructed to take all the furniture in the house and put it into a pile in the front room. Then we had to put it back. What seemed like an arduous and arbitrary activity managed to completely reanimate the house, so that for the rest of our time in that space we were connected to it, had handled and placed each piece of furniture, prayed for its safe transport, knew its texture and weight intimately.

The point in writing to you about all this is not to expound on the philosophies of the school I started or to tell you to follow your dreams. The position of the Oracle at Delphi was at the center of one of the most powerful religious institutions in Ancient Greece; her role sat at the center of incredible amounts of power and wealth. She did not disappear when her religion was outlawed and her temple closed. We still talk about her two thousand years later. In

Heroditus's *Histories*, the Oracle at Delphi proclaimed, *"I know the number of the sand and the measure of the sea; I understand the speech of the dumb and hear the voiceless."* To know things of this magnitude, she must have seen in herself a deep connection.o have a mind the measure of an ocean she would then *be* the ocean.

The Corpus Hermeticum, a Hellenstic text dated to around the 1st century CE, was written while the Oracle at Delphi still lived and worked. It's structured as a dialogue between the god Hermes and a student. When the student asks Hermes how he might know god the answer was this:

> If then you do not make yourself equal to God, you cannot apprehend God; for like is known by like . . . Think that for you too nothing is impossible; deem that you too are immortal, and that you are able to grasp all things in your thought, to know every craft and science; find your home in the haunts of every living creature; make yourself higher than all heights and lower than all depths; bring together in yourself all opposites of quality, heat and cold, dryness and fluidity; think that you are everywhere at once, on land, at sea, in heaven; think that you are not yet begotten, that you are in the womb, that you are young, that you are old, that you have died, that you are in the world beyond the grave; grasp in your thought all of this at once, all times and places, all substances and qualities and magnitudes together; then you can apprehend God.

What the voice in the ground at Delphi gave me when I thought I had nothing was connection, and the determination to maintain a connection that requires both listening and responding. If I could hear the voices of these dead prophets in the ground, then I was both the dead prophet and the ground. In a "nothing special" kind of way. If we can turn toward ourselves and each other now, turn toward the skies and seas, then we see that magic is alive and we can know that nothing is impossible.

Witching, Weaving, Casting Spells toward Liberation

A CONVERSATION WITH
adrienne maree brown and Dori Midnight

Introduction

Across time and place, witches have often gathered on the edges, in the dark, in the wilds, and in our homes. Much of our wisdom has been passed down, not through formal teaching or written guidebooks, but through story and song, gossip and whisper, practice, doing and undoing, and real talk at the well, the street corner, in the bathroom at the conference, and at the kitchen table.

This conversation, conducted over Zoom and later transcribed, between adrienne maree brown and Dori Midnight, two writers/healers/thinkers, is inspired by the tradition/practice/magic of friendship, and the wisdom that emerges and is caught when listening in on a conversation. adrienne and Dori have known each other for decades, circling around each other in both organizing realms and witchy ways, supporting and being supported by each other's work. In this conversation, adrienne and Dori both weave and are woven into the temporal braids of relational magic, as two witches working to cast spells toward a liberated future.

What Is a Witch?

Witching, Weaving, Casting Spells
Toward Liberation

DORI MIDNIGHT

Here we are, two middle aged witches talking about witching. adrienne, I'm curious, how do you relate to and understand the word "witch?"

ADRIENNE MAREE BROWN

A witch is someone who engages with the natural world, including the human body, with healing and magical intentions. Like, I am going to use this mugwort to do something inside my system. I'm going to send out a spell to shift what's possible in the universe right now, trusting that everything that is alive can feel that spell. Or when I send my spells out through the Internet, I'm creating a wave, hopefully, of some laughter and some joy and some peace and some understanding in the midst of a hard life, a hard time.

I feel very conscious of the way that I'm partnering with the human body, with the soma, with the human being on the other side of—often—a digital communication, because I'm a witch of my time. Often I'm reaching through the digital and the human body which is always a nature-space. This space wants to give life to the part of you that craves life. When I call out my song, I need to hear the song sung back to me. My body is part of the offer, and it's about being in relationship with what is. What a miracle. What about you?

DM

Yes, I feel so much how we are relational witches practicing relational witchcraft—in service to life, in service to mutual flourishing, and also in service to death, as part of life. This is where it is at for me, especially in this time of so much destruction and despair and unraveling. Racial capitalism so voraciously forecloses upon life and upon our connection to life and our life-giving ways (while also promoting only a certain narrow kind of life) and in that, creates so much disenchantment and disconnection to source and magic. It is through this wild pulse, the way life calls to life through us and in us, that we invite each other back into wildness, back into magic. We re-enchant these traditions, in the literal sense of that word: renewing incantations, breathing life back into something, in collaboration with everything, because *we are* collaborations. For me, witching is profoundly relational, it's a love practice, it's being in service to what I love, which is life itself, in and across and out of time and space.

AMB

I often talk about this idea that there's a rope thrown back from the future that you can grab onto. You can choose to take the one that leads you toward joy and abundance, toward a world that doesn't have the norms or borders that we currently live inside of, to a world where humans are bringing each other delight and in right relationship with the land. So, I'm pulling on that, and I don't even know if it's a spell or just like, "Come with me, come on." This is the thread, right? Everything around us is inevitably going to collapse because it's built on faulty, traumatic ground. When the things that were built on slavery, inequality, and capitalism go away, we can hold on to each other and find ourselves in a new formation.

DM

Yes, I think we have to be casting spells toward new ways, toward liberation, as much as we need to break spells, to hasten the inevitable collapse of these structures of subjugation. Spells are woven things. (I'm also feeling the ways you and I toss words like golden thread back and forth.) Witches are all about textiles—we collect and make magic with scraps, we tie knots, we weave with the invisible, we love rope and shrouds and scarves, we tend to the fabric of life and death. And when I close my eyes, I see with my witch eyes the web that *we are* the web of care and magic that we make with each other. And how we change the fabric of the universe with our spell work—unraveling and binding and breaking and weaving anew, from the old. And the lineages of witchcraft certainly feel like a rope from the past and future to me—one that cannot be severed, though sometimes it can feel lost or far away. That tug, that pull also feels like intuition. Magic for me has always been about deep listening. A deep and wide listening to everything. Like what even is my intuition but something, everything singing through me? How do we know what we know? I think probably by unknowing a lot of things, including our separateness.

———

AMB

When I think about intuition, the challenge for me has been trusting that if I ask for support, if I ask for the Earth to hold me, if I ask my ancestors to come, they would know how to even hear me, that they would listen to me. I recently put on this musical ritual. Before the ritual, I asked the Benevolent Ancestors to come in, to come and be a part of this space. And then we had invited this priestess, and she shows up, she sings in her language and then tells us that she asked the ancestors to come into the room and protect us. We never told her to do that—she just knew. And when I was meditating before the ritual, I was singing a song: "Ancestors, come into the room with us. Benevolent ancestors come, come into the room." And I felt them enter and realized, oh you're really available. I didn't know how much I've longed to know that and how much I have been reaching for them. And then my usual fear of singing went away and I sang. It was like, who cares what you sound like right now? This is about the choir singing.

I grew up in, "You pray to God, God's not going to answer you directly in that kind of way." But the witchy way of being in relationship to ancestors and the divine feels so different from that. I expect to feel the connection in return.

I have a lot of humility because of that. I don't know with my head at all what I'm supposed to be doing. Like, I'm smart, I'm articulate, whatever. The way comes up from the body, it comes up from the sacrum, it comes up from my pelvic area.

Yes! I love this story about how we know what we know through our bodies, which also reveals a deeper, longer story about how oppressive, or maybe suppressive, forces and structures have long undermined our knowing and our trust in our own knowing, attempting to sever our connections from our bodies, from land, from each other, our bodies as bodies of earth. All as source and resource, intuition as attunement to all of this. And for me, my intuition also moves like desire, like a sparkling hum of "yes" inside. I've learned to trust my desire and follow it like a lantern. In my practice, doing healing work with people, I really try to pour honey on that longing and let the longing be a guide. *And* it has gotten so intertwined with fear and disappointment and shame and pain. But damn, our desire for connection is the prayer. When people come to me with so much yearning—for ancestors, for connection, for magic, for wisdom, for remembering something so deep, I'm like, *yes!* Follow that yearning! Be hungry and go find it!

I think when we allow our desire to rise up, when we give it space to breathe, it can move us, urge us toward the thing. I think of it as a wild prayer, like a weed. Desire becomes, or is itself, a prayer. Spells are poems, and also spells are the wellsprings of desire, and also like flowers reaching toward light. Water these desire flowers with love, give them our attention, and that becomes the practice, the craft. Do it with other people, and that grows community and trust and care. Because magic *is* relational, magic *is* a poetic practice of presence and attention and intention. I think of that Diane di Prima poem, about learning to trust yourself and the magic *when it works.*

―――
AMB

Yes! I'm someone who needs evidence, so I don't do any practices when I don't have evidence that they are working right. Oh, if tarot cards were not on point all the time, I wouldn't pull tarot cards. Yesterday was a wild day, but the Chani astro app had already told me it's going to be this way specifically, and here's what to remind yourself of to move through it. And I laugh because people are just out here moving through the world without tarot and astrology and therapy, and I'm astounded. I'm just like, what? How?

It's rough out there without it! Rawdogging it through life without magic and without each other! Yikes.

It's rough if you don't have the tools, but again, it's evidence. I see distinctly that my life is better when I do these things. And then I think about the other piece of witchcraft around desire and longing and prayer, and a couple of thoughts came up as you were talking.

Everyone knows how to pray when there's a crisis. It comes so quickly, like "I think that someone I love is dead. Please, G-d, no. Please, somebody. I will trade my life for that person. I will stop this behavior. . . " We immediately have a sense of surrender.

When that happens, I'm willing to change how I am, some fundamental aspects of how I am or what I consider to be my fatal flaw if only something can intervene and stop this from happening. We have an inner sense of preventative knowing and reactive knowing. We have a sense of reactive knowing how to connect to spirit and that our bodies matter and our behaviors really matter. We believe that. So much of being a witch is going preventative with that knowledge. If we can apply this technology under duress, what is it like to look ahead and think, if you lay these seeds in the ground, if you plant these spells, if you engage in this way of clearing your energy and doing your spiritual hygiene, you don't have to get to the crisis point.

I think about all the people that I've lost lately. There's a level of spiritual hygiene that you need to survive the world right now. And many of us don't learn it until it's too late, until the toxicity of the world has already rooted in our systems. By the time they were able to reach the spaciousness, the top of whatever mountain in life, they finally realized like, I can take a breath. I could stop here and pause and look back down the hill and see what I've come through. That's self-reflection.

I always tell people it's a privilege to have any space and time to self-reflect. Being a witch is saying, I have time. I reflect, and I have time to not reflect just for myself, but for that collective desire. When I reflect, what I can feel is there's so much longing for things to be different than they are right now.

DM

Yes, and I think there's a fine line between magic (by which I mean specifically working or bending or weirding time and space, anchoring our intentions, and casting spells) and the terrible, sad illusion that we are in control, which is also tricky territory because it's fertile ground for blame and/or self-blame. I think racial capitalism and, well, don't get me started on the enlightenment and the destruction of the commons, but I think for so many of us there's been a profound loss of connection to a culture of community care *as* a spritual practice, which I think is what being a witch is all about. And because there is so much vulnerablity and precarity for so many people, and not enough care and real solidarity and connection, sometimes the hunger for magic, for a lineage of practice, for protection, for wisdom, for togetherness, makes us kind of desperate. And materialism fucks us up into thinking we can buy our way into magic, get our hands on some sparkly thing will keep us safe or in control.

As someone who makes potions and crafts amulets, who sits with people every day experiencing grief and pain and trauma, who is in the work or practice or poetry of healing, I understand these makings and doings and deep listening to be part of tending to the web of life. And when I make someone an amulet, I do it as an anti-materialist witch. The amulet is a visble, tangible thing, but a thing is not magic in itself. The magic is in what the thing points to, which is invisible, which I guess one could call care, or love, or interdependence, or the web we're held within. It's both infused with this care ("I made this for you, something flowed from my heart into my hands!") and a physical, embodied reminder of that care. A thing made with love and time locates us within this luminous network, transmits a sense of connection, which *is* magic. Hold an amulet and you feel held, you remember yourself as part of something that extends way beyond yourself. The amulet transmits a sense of kinship, belonging, and care. The way we are tied to and responsible for one another.

Healing rituals are relational magic and rigourous magic. They are like the fruiting body of the mycelial web of care. Rituals generate and strengthen the web, and are one way we map this web of connection. We call on magic as a devotional expression of collective care to mend the web of life (a mending and a life that includes and honors dying and the dead), life supporting life. Witching is not about trying to control outcome or to prevent bad things from happening, which, unfortunately we cannot do. But it is more like a daily practice of multidirectional collective care because hard things *are* always happening. It makes sense to me that so many of our tools are quotidian things or scraps or found things: water, flame, seeds, circles, metal, thread, stones, a pot, a strand of hair. We sweep as daily psychic hygiene, we touch the earth to ground, we drench ourselves in honey to sweeten our spirits. We actually have everything we need. So I always ask people who are hungry for more magic: what are you doing that's already a ritual, that's already magic? How can you bring more attention and purpose into what you're doing without being too precious about it, without overefforting? And I encourage people to make messes, make mistakes, let life flow, to not know. Shit is going to happen, so the prayer can't be for nothing ever to happen! We are alive in this great unraveling. And we fucking need magic.

The Spells We Cast, the Spells We Break

What are the spells you are casting these days?

One of the core spells moving through me is for us to get back in touch with our wildness in some way. I keep telling people to go put their feet in the dirt in the backyard. I think it helps if we want to grow our aliveness, to pay attention to it, to be like—the tree in my backyard is precious. I'm not going to take it for granted. I'm going to care for it and let it care for me and hold me when I need holding. I think if we let the relationships between us and what is wild around us die, it puts everything that's alive at risk. The world is in relationship with us, we are in relationship with the world and that should guide how we're in relationship with each other and ourselves.

There's also a major spell about being in relationship to our death and to mortality and to grief. I was just counting yesterday that in the last six months, I've lost five people that I loved at different points in my life. They were teachers, they were all peers within ten years of me. And they were all unexpected. I can try to run from that, or I can reflect on why they're not here anymore and how my life is as precious and precarious as any of theirs. And how do I want to live given that reality? My relationship with death puts me into direct relationship with joy, connection, honesty, and just being like, it's fucking today. This is the day that we definitely have right now. I don't know how much time we have so if it's on my schedule, it's something I would want to do if this was my last day. That orientation feels like a spell for my life.

And of course, pleasure is a major spell in my life. Letting the good be good, letting as much of the good be good and feel good, and learning how to enjoy the parts of humanity that make life worth living even in an apocalyptic time.

That's both powerful spell casting and also spell breaking, to cultivate and center pleasure and goodness and beauty as things fall apart. And it's a big undoing inside of ourselves especially in the world of changemakers and activism, a world in which we're taught to center and lead from/with suffering. Both you and I came up as witches in organizing work. I was holding healing spaces and dosing people with potions and teaching psychic hygiene magic in movement spaces for decades. I know that's also a huge part of your journey as a witch and as an activist. So, how do we cast spells with our life force toward the world we want and find ways to lead and vision and move from a new, more resourced, pleasure seeking place?

AMB

As an organizer, protester, and activist, a lot of the energy was casting a spell of, "No, that's what I don't want." I've shifted my energy to manifesting what I do want and then figuring out how to practice that on any given Thursday afternoon. Awakening is a lifelong process and it's about how we shape the conditions around us. Even if I think I have no power, I have the power to impact the people around me, and that's a huge power that can create bonds of desire and longing, and those bonds can create community that's built around a shared willingness to practice something new.

DM

It's making me think about how witch work is also a practice of resistance. Witches have always been part of a sacred refusal to participate in systems and structures of dominance and control. Witches have so much to offer in terms of practicing new worlds, practicing new ways, imagining and dreaming unimaginable possibilities that are also deeply rooted in the old. What do you think it is about witches that makes us so good at that?

We're not afraid of shadows. We're not afraid of the dark side of the moon. We're not afraid of even dark eras or dark times. Most of the witches I know have a sense of there always being a balance of these things in life. There's always something being born at the same time something is dying. And the portals are very similar. So, I think witch work can offer presence. Like, what that person is learning or what these folks are going through is actually a part of their journey. We're going to look back at this period. Someone will look back at this period and be able to see very clearly, oh, there was a whole seventy million strong portion of this nation that was caught up in some very deluded beliefs.

But there's something that this country is trying to learn on behalf of the species as well. One of the lessons is that racial capitalism doesn't work, right? Living out of connection with the Earth doesn't work, but it's on a larger scale. It's never failure, but always a lesson. Witches get this—like okay, that spell showed me that that's not the spell. Next time, I'm not going to put the essence of butterflies in that spell. Got to put something else in it.

On the larger scale, witches believe in second chances, especially for people who have been brainwashed or gaslit. There's something hard that your soul has to figure out that my soul actually does seem to know right now, even if there are a lot of other things my soul doesn't know.

I think writing fables is a place where I get to really play with generating new stories in this world. I get to make sense of what it would be like for these people to make it to the other side.

—
DM

I think about how witching is a craft, how we are *crafty*. We craft with our hands and our words. In Jewish tradition, it is quite literal that words create worlds. And in turn, we can also unmake with our words, unravel the fabric of the universe, and spin new tales from old thread.

You are literally a fabulist, a weaver of story magic! When I close my eyes and listen/dream, I see you sitting at a loom and the threads are starlight and mycelium—that's always how I see you when you are writing.

Witch work is also a wide cosmic listening work. I think this is my main work, which I suppose can also be called channeling. I need to keep the ears of my heart, my intuition, clear as a golden bell so I can hear clearly. I listen to the stories of the spheres, to the stories under the earth, to the revolt of the orcas, the grief songs of the whales, and to people. What I mean by listening also includes seeing. I listen to a collective thrum and peek at some shimmering web thing. And I tend to what is broken, what is hurting, what is in need of remedy. I make a prayer every day to let my ears and heart and hands be used by whatever you want to call it—god, life, eros, creation, magic, love.

I'm grateful to come from a tradition that has hundreds of names for the divine and not a lot of need to figure it out, so I don't get tripped up in trying to. I rarely attempt to explain what I do, which is why these interviews are sometimes like an existential trip for me. But I guess this work is really about being available for connection and intimacy and change and healing and relating in infinite directions.

AMB

I always say, I'm going to make myself available and put myself in the way of magic. So I'm constantly making myself available. Maybe I'm in a conversation—and hold on, I just need to pick up my phone and write down something because the song lyric just came. If the Universe wants to give it to me, I'm going to be here for it. Whether it's God or the ancestors, or lived experience, or the scientific method, all of these ways of knowing feel like different ways of getting to the wisdom.

And the work of witching is, to me, a way I can harness knowledge and energy and make new worlds. I think of Harriet Tubman a lot—I can shape more freedom for people who are interested in freedom. I can't make anyone be free who's not interested in that. But if you're interested in freedom, I can point you in the right direction. I can walk with you and be like, don't eat those berries across the river, or this is a good place to cross the river. If you chew this and stick it on your wound, it'll heal faster.

This is a great training in which to learn how to be in your body a bit more. I received flowers after some loved ones passed and I put them around a tree in my backyard which is now an energetic cemetery. Being around a tree is meaningful and humans gathering around a tree is a healing thing. It's why lynching is such a violation. Trees want to be a part of gathering, coming together, spreading roots, and holding on. There are things we just know.

—

DM

Yes, how much of what we do is just being breathed and moved by the ancestors; like we're just their doings? I think about how so many diasporic people have hidden our wisdom, hidden jewels, hidden seeds—in our pockets, our hair, our books. Hiding magical traditions inside of religious practice, hiding witching in the daily kitchen tasks, in our home-tending. So much of witch work is about remembering what we already know, and also being willing to not know, being willing to be shaped by life, to love mystery, to be marked by loss, to be moved by and in love with plants and stones and wind and water.

—

AMB

For a long time, I struggled with the willingness to be shaped. Sometimes I'm like, I got good at this thing already, so now I'm good at this thing. Multiple times in my life, I've had to remember that it doesn't matter if you put a lot of time and effort into getting good at that thing. That was just teaching you one aspect of a skill that wasn't the whole shebang, and you're meant to be shaped for some other purpose that's larger than yourself. And I don't mean that I'm shaped by people who can see me. I'm being shaped by something unseen that is meant to show up for the people who can see me in the same way.

To me, this means I have to say, yes, I'm a witch. We have been burned, but this is what I was called to do. And yes, I'm a singer. I don't sing perfectly, but I have to sing because that's what I was told to do. And yes, I am a perfectionist, and I'm going to now make a bunch of mistakes in public and call it a life and write about it and reflect and share it, because that's what I was called to do. I'm sure there are more uncomfortable tasks ahead of me, including the fact that I will die, and I would rather not.

I am so into life. I love being alive, and I love the tangible, pleasurable experiences of life, but I can already feel my body deteriorating and starting the move away from life. I'm not into it, but it's also going to have to happen, and then that death will bring something to others, right? By surrendering to the parts that have to be, I can ask then, what's the pleasure inside of this? It feels incredible when you surrender to what you're supposed to be doing. Yeah, I learn in public. I laugh—oh, flubbed it up again. When I learn, the more people who are watching me, the more people learn with me at the very same moment. Now I have so much less shame and less guilt. I'm not even a perfectionist anymore, because that's not a human thing. That's something else.

———

DM

What a time to be alive! I am so into it, even though life basically breaks my heart every day. But getting older is such a blessing! I am also loving feeling more and more free from shame and guilt, I'm pretty into the wild ride of perimenopause, and I'm also excited to be compost and flowers someday, honestly. And I'm so glad to be in this witch work with you.

———

AMB

Me too. I wouldn't have it any other way. Bless!

CONTRIBUTOR BIOS

adrienne maree brown grows healing ideas in public through her multi-genre writing, her music and her podcasts. Informed by twenty-five years of movement facilitation, somatics, Octavia E Butler scholarship, and her work as a doula, adrienne has nurtured Emergent Strategy, Pleasure Activism, Radical Imagination and Transformative Justice as ideas and practices for transformation. She is the author/editor of several texts including *Fables and Spells* and *Pleasure Activism,* cogenerator of *The Liberation Tarot Deck,* and a developing musical ritual.

Aja Daashuur is a leading light whose name is synonymous with spiritual elevation and profound connection, renowned for her transformative influence in the wellness and sacred healing realms. She is the Spirit Guide Coach, a medium, and a certified past life regression integrator, offering her gifts at sacred venues across the country. Her intuitive coaching and channeling process is deeply intertwined with the wisdom of her Spirit Guides, empowering individuals to shatter negative cycles, embrace their true path, and revel in the ceaseless love and support that the spiritual realm offers. Aja's impact extends far beyond individual consultations; she is the visionary founder of Spirit House Collective, one of the first BIPOC female-led wellness communities in Los Angeles. Under her guidance, the Collective has hosted over 500 workshops, carving out a much-needed inclusive and diverse space for both the marginalized and the spiritually curious. With accolades and features in *Vogue, The Cut, The LA Times, Mind Body Green,* and numerous other publications, Aja stands as one of the most renowned mediums and spiritual guides on the West Coast. Through her forthcoming oracle decks, books, and spiritually enriching classes, she continues to widen the corridors of understanding, fostering a global connection to the wealth of love and wisdom that our Spirit Guides hold for us.

Alejandra Luisa León is a Tarot reader, astrologer, writer and artist. She is the creatrix of three hand collaged divination decks: *The Lioness Oracle Tarot, Vision of the Muse,* and *The Stars Divine.* She has taught classes, given hundreds of readings, and continues to learn the art of magic. Her art practice began as a way to work with grief and continues to be a healing modality.

Amanda Yates Garcia is a writer and public witch. Her work has been featured in *The New York Times, The LA Times, The SF Chronicle, The London Times,* CNN, BRAVO, as well as a viral appearance on FOX. She has led rituals, classes and workshops on magic and witchcraft at UCLA, UC Irvine, MOCA, the Hammer Museum, LACMA, the Getty, and many other venues. Amanda hosts monthly moon rituals online, and the popular *Between the Worlds* podcast, which looks at the Western Mystery traditions through a mythopoetic lens. Her book, *Initiated: Memoir of a Witch,* received a starred review from Kirkus and Publisher's Weekly and has been translated into six languages. To find out more about her work visit her Substack, Mystery Cult with Amanda Yates Garcia. *substack.com/@amandayatesgarcia*

Angela Mary Magick (She/They) is the creatrix of *Moon bb Magick Tarot, Altalune Sensual Oracle Cards,* and host of *Venus Between Us* video podcast on YouTube. Find their Worldwide Coven on YouTube, Patreon Witchcraft Club, Instagram, and their newsletter love note. Angela is a Witch, mama, emergent artist, community organizer, educator, lifelong student ASMRtist, ceremony officiant, aromatherapy and beauty professional. Angela Mary Magick is incredibly honored to have been the FemmeCee of Modern Witches Confluence on Halloween 2021.

Ariella Daly is a dream weaver, bee tender, mother, musician, witch, and facilitator. Devoted to the bee in both the physical world and the spirit world, she beautifully synthesizes natural beekeeping, animism, dream work, nature connection, and embodiment through writing, retreats, and classes.

Ariella has over twenty-five years' experience designing, leading, and participating in earth-centric workshops and ceremonies. She is trained in a European animistic spiritual pathway, often called bee shamanism, with the honeybee and the serpent as its central motifs. Within this pathway, she is versed in healing, womb shamanism, oracular seership, and dream incubation.

Her work combines firsthand knowledge of the honeybee species with an intimate understanding of bee shamanism. Ariella seeks to foster a deeper relationship between humans and the natural world through honeybees, and sees the bee as a bridge species between our domestic lives and the wild, both within and around us. She is a lover of wild places, liminal spaces, and the song of the land.

Aurora Luna, aka Baby Reckless is a multiple disciplinary artist whose work focuses on self-actualization, myth, mystery, the occult, and gender. Their work includes music, prints, collages, films, and graphic arts. They believe that by working in harmony with the elements, seasons, and stars, and embracing ourselves entirely, we can create our own kind of magic. They continue to make magic in their art as they explore their own vision through multiple mediums.

Not only a full-time artist, Baby Reckless is a writer and oracle/astrologer (Western and Jyotish) whose work is heavily informed and influenced by myth, magic and mystery. Through practice and patronage, they are able to reach audiences virtually and actualize their goal of their art being a vehicle and a tool to help others like them on that very personal hero's journey.

Baby Reckless is a visionary based in NYC, LA, and Dallas. On any given day they can be found bringing new worlds to life through the use of magic, music, and their paint brushes.

Damiana Calvario is a mixed woman of color, daughter, sister, caregiver, community member, survivor, first generation immigrant. Her practice blends together her Mexican roots, mixed upbringing, food as medicine, *curanderismo* studies, and Western herbalism training, rooted in care work and mutual aid.

Dori Midnight is a community care worker, ritual artist, theologian, writer, and deep listener oriented toward collective healing and liberation. For over two decades, Dori has woven rituals and practiced intuitive, community-based healing in one-on-one sessions and in radical movement spaces, in collaboration with the seen and unseen, plants, stones, stories, and more. Dori offers workshops on rituals and remedies for unraveling times, re-enchanting Jewish ancestral wisdoms as a liberatory practice, and queer magic and healing. Supported and inspired by a wide web of dreamers, witches, artists, and web workers, Dori's work is rooted in feminist, decolonial and abolitionist scholarship, queer liberation, and disability and healing justice work. Dori has been in deep cahoots with movement work for Palestinian liberation, prison abolition, and queer and trans liberation based in racial and economic justice for over twenty years. Dori lives on the occupied lands of the Pocumtuc and Nipmuc, by the Quinnehtukqut River, also known as Northampton, Massachusetts.

Edgar Fabián Frías is a boundary-breaking multidisciplinary artist based in LA. Their work blends diverse artistic disciplines, challenging conventional categories. Frías explores resiliency and radical imagination through Indigenous Futurism, spirituality, and queer aesthetics. *www.edgarfabianfrias.org*

Eliza Swann, aka Emerald is an interdisciplinary artist, intuitive, writer, and educator based in New York City. Eliza received a BA in Painting from the San Francisco Art Institute and an MFA from Central St. Martins in London. They studied hypnotherapy at the Isis Centre, Vedic cosmology with Dr. Vagish Shastri, Insight Meditation with the Insight Meditation Society, and ancestral healing with Daniel Foor. They are an initiate of orders belonging to Gnostic Christian and Hermetic traditions. Eliza has exhibited artwork internationally, most recently at the University of California Santa Cruz (Santa Cruz, CA), and the Feminist Center for Creative Work (Los Angeles, CA). Eliza has contributed writing to *BOMB, Arthur, Contemporary Art Review LA, Momus,* and *Perfect Wave.* Their book, *The Anatomy of the Aura,* was released by St. Martin's

Press in April 2020. Eliza is the founder of The Golden Dome School and currently teaches alchemy at Pratt Institute.

Jessie Susannah Karnatz, aka the Money Witch, brings capitalism-critical, shame-free education to healers, hustlers, and creatives in order to catalyze change in their financial lives. She believes healing our finances will bring blessing to our lives, our lineages, and our communities. She offers education, Money Magic products, and intuitive financial coaching online from the Bay Area (unceded Ohlone land) and does it all with impeccable business lady style.

Jessie Susannah is the cult leader at Money Coven, an online web of magical beings who are healing their relationship with money, showing up for their financial self-care, and becoming powerful stewards to their resources. You can find more information on her work at *moneywitch.com*

Jezmina Von Thiele (they/she) is a writer, educator, and fortune teller in their mixed Romani tradition. They write poetry, fiction, and nonfiction published in Prairie Schooner, The Kenyon Review Online, Narrative Magazine, and elsewhere, often under the name Jessica Reidy. Jezmina also teaches online and in-person classes and workshops on literature, writing, creativity, magical self-care, and divination. They read tarot, palms, and tea leaves online and in-person at Deadwick's Ethereal Emporium in Portsmouth, NH. Jezmina also tells fortunes and performs with The Poetry Brothel—Boston. They are co-host of *Romanistan,* a podcast celebrating Romani culture, alongside co-host Paulina Stevens. Paulina and Jezmina are also writing a book on Romani fortune telling expected to be published in the fall of 2024 with Weiser. Jezmina is also owner and operator of the online vintage Etsy shop, Evil Eye Edit.

Kiki Robinson, aka Opulent Witch (they/them) I am a tarot reader, multimedia artist, dancer, healing arts practitioner, and co-creator of The Living Altar along with Ylva Mara Radziszewski. I am a queer and nonbinary practicing witch of traditional magic. My altar is centered in sovereignty, justice and compassion. My ancestral background is Irish, British Isles, and Romani. My first love of magic came through art of many mediums including printmaking, dance and performance art, and my intention is to embody healing and magic through my Creative Spirit. I live on unceded Chinook land, now known as Portland, OR.

Kimberly Rodriguez (She/Her/Ella), also known as Poeta Goddess, is an Indigenous Mexican illustrator, poet, and author. Kimberly's work weaves the intention of connection, healing, and resistance as an act to live by the truth of who we are. You can follow her work over on Instagram @poetagoddess and *www .poetagoddess.com*

Liz Migliorelli belongs to a lineage of bee maidens, apple romancers, and herb cunning-folk. She is a clinical herbalist, educator and animist who roots her work in the stories and practices of her ancestors. Her people are Neapolitan, Campanian, Western Slavic from the Tatra mountains, Anglo-Saxon, and Gaul. She lives in the Hudson Valley of New York on Munsee-Esopus-Lenape lands where she tends to a garden and apple orchard. She sings to flowers, grows a lot of garlic, and makes regular offerings to the snakes and other land spirits that are in the neighborhood. She is fiercely devoted to enchantment in all realms. Her favorite divination tools are beeswax, murky waters, and chickens.

Her work as a clinical and community herbalist involves medicinal herbs, flower essences, and personal ritual in a harm-reduction framework. She also offers a line of flower essences under the name Sister Spinster and believes flower essences are some of the most potent medicines for our times. Liz has been teaching classes on mythopoetic herbalism, ancestral remembrance, folk magic, and storytelling for over ten years. She will always be a student of the plants. You can learn more about her work at *www.sisterspinster.net*

Madre Jaguar is a Curandera, Clairvoyant Oracle, Birth Doula and Intuitive Artist.

Madre Jaguar has always walked between the worlds. Ever since they can remember, Madre Jaguar has experienced visions, prophetic dreams, visitations and a strong clear connection to their Spirit team. They are the child of

Salvadoran immigrants; of Nahuatl, Mayan, Pipil, and Garifuna descent, born in Los Angeles, California and raised in Mexico, where they currently reside.

A passion for helping others and a strong desire to propel positive change in the world, led Madre Jaguar on a path of self-discovery, reclaiming of ancestral practices and the exploration of different healing modalities including Curanderismo, Reiki and Energy Healing, Shamanic Practices, Folk Magic, Herbalism and Tarot. They have studied with indigenous healers and teachers in Mexico, Central and South America.

Madre Jaguar believes that Love is our super power. As human beings we are here to bless and be blessed by all of creation. Harmony and Joy are our birthright. Through their healing practice, readings, classes and projects Madre Jaguar's goal is to help you connect with the inner power, wisdom and magic that lies within.

Maria Minnis is a Black, Jewish, queer, and autistic tarot reader of twenty plus years who teaches people about blending their spirituality with magic, liberation work, and eroticism in their everyday lives. She believes that the end result of all magic should be to cultivate a more equitable and empathetic planet. Her highly praised antiracism tarot workbook *Tarot for the Hard Work* is available online and in stores.

Olivia Ephraim Pepper (flexible pronouns) is a queer, unschooled, mixed heritage mystic and lifelong poet whose work with star poetry, Tarot, and magic spans several decades after being gifted a childhood that allowed for the development of a spiritual self.

Born in a hand-built cabin with no running water or electricity, Olivia genuinely wasn't sure what century they were living in until the age of thirteen (having assumed it was the 24th because that's what they said on *Star Trek*). Olivia is also a trained herbalist, mortality awareness advocate, assemblage artist, retired puppeteer, reluctant memelord, and occasional experimental filmmaker—essentially a professional ditherer who is diligently practicing enchantment. Olivia is passionate about art, abolitionism, disability theory, folklore, absurdist comedy, and decolonial history. Dream dinner party guests include: Leonora Carrington, James Baldwin, Maria Tallchief, Octavia Butler, John Trudell, Ursula K. LeGuin, h.d., Herman Hesse, Frantz Fanon, Claude Cahun, and bell hooks.

Rachel Howe is an illustrator, a writer, a Tarot and astrology practitioner and scholar, a hand-poke tattoo artist, a certified hypnotherapist, and a certified Reiki Master. She founded Small Spells—an interdisciplinary, multi-dimensional brand, inspired by mysticism and linking together esoteric healing and contemporary design—over a decade ago. Small Spells specializes in creating hand-drawn illustrations, books, and objects that are inspired by mysticism, magic, and nature. The studio's work is often characterized by bold, minimal lines, and a playful aesthetic. Rachel also offers workshops, classes, and individual Tarot and astrology readings focused on creative expression, self-care, and personal growth. Her writings, primarily on astrology and investigations of healing concepts, combine channeled timeless wisdom with a grounded and modern perspective. After growing up in New Jersey, and spending most of her adult life in New York City, she is now based in Los Angeles. She considers herself a private solitary witch who works to support the empowerment of all people to engage in the web of life in the ways that best suit them, free from oppression.

Sanyu Estelle is a claircognizant ("clear knowing") Soothsayer ("truth teller") that is also known as "the Word Witch" because of her deep love for word origins (etymology) and word culture (philology). As a Soothsayer, Sanyu Estelle's gift is truth telling. With eleven years of card reading experience, fifteen years of workshop experience, and twenty-five years of public speaking experience, her readings are often listened to over many years by her clients for even further insight. In addition to soothsaying and card readings, Sanyu Estelle also teaches workshops and cohorts on dreaming, ancestral research, Tarot reading and history, and her own methodology called "Quantum Energetics"; a praxis that instructs people on how to use their emotional, intellectual, physical and spiritual intelligences as a living divination system. Sanyu Estelle is currently the resident card reader at Soho Warehouse in Los Angeles and has had her writing published or featured by *The New York Times,* Sarah Faith Gottesdiener's *Many Moons Lunar Planner,* the Feminist Center for Creative Work's *Salima Magazine,* Row House Publishing, and the Geffen Contemporary Warehouse at MOCA.

Star Feliz is not just a spiritual guide; they are a transformational portal between humanity and the Earth, channeling the spirit of plants to bring about profound healing. Descended from the Afro-Taino *cimarrónes* of the Bahoruco Mountains in the Dominican Republic, Star carries the wisdom of generations, inherited from stories passed down by their mother and grandmother. With over a decade of expertise in herbal practices, queer birthwork, and movements for radical liberation, Star has empowered countless individuals to reconnect with their ancestral roots and discover their personal power.

In 2020, Star launched Botánica Cimarrón, a treasure trove of handcrafted, organic plant medicines and unique ritual tools, created on the ancestral lands of the Tongva and Gabrielino peoples in Los Angeles. This space offers a myriad of ways to embark on a journey of cosmic Earth healing. One standout creation is the *Green Gold: An Ancestral Plant Spirit Oracle Deck,* a transformative tool that has already received critical acclaim from Architectural Digest, the Los Angeles Times, and Taschen's Library of Esoterica series. But Star's genius doesn't stop there; they are also an accomplished multidisciplinary artist, known by the moniker Priestusssy. From experimental devotional music to ground-breaking installations, Star's artistic gifts span sound, sculpture, film, and more, all aimed at challenging and reshaping our collective psyche. Their recent book, *When Eye Land,* interrogates colonial perspectives and has solidified Star's standing as an influential cultural thought leader. Whether through art, music, or ancestral wisdom, Star Feliz offers myriad avenues for you to reclaim your own power and purpose.

About the Editor

At home in the overlooked intersections of dreams, meadows, and used book-shops, Casey Zabala has always known herself as a witch, hedge-walker, and weaver between worlds. Having been gifted her first tarot deck for her thirteenth birthday, Casey began her occult and magical studies early on, and her fixation with enchantment has been a strong thread through her life and work ever since. Her illustrated and authored divinatory tools include *Wanderer's Tarot*, *Wanderer's Tarot Guidebook*, and *Wyrd Sisters Oracle*. In 2018 Casey founded Modern Witches, and hosted her first Modern Witches Confluence; a symposium for seekers and witches featuring presentations from notable witches, including Starhawk, over Samhain weekend. Modern Witches continues to host educational spiritual gatherings, and Casey hosts the Modern Witches Podcast. Casey's life and work aims to uplift the healing power of witchcraft, particularly as we face unprecedented planetary crises. Currently living in Northern California, you will find Casey wandering through the forests, baking bread, offering oracular counsel, and making art in collaboration with her spirit helpers.

About Modern Witches

We strive to cultivate a radical, liberatory, diverse, and inclusive magical community of being who believe in healing futures and in the crucial role witches play in healthy societies. Founded in 2018 by Casey Zabala, Modern Witches started off as a dream to bring a diverse and radical group of magical beings together. Modern Witches came to life via a Confluence gathering at the San Francisco County Fair Building, organized by Casey, complete with a craft fair featuring witch-owned businesses, and magical presentations from famous witches and a keynote address from Starhawk. The event has continued on annually since then, and has expanded its offerings into the virtual realm. Over the years, the Modern Witches community has grown, yet it remains a community rooted in authentic spirituality, radical education, and social justice. We believe that the archetype of the witch holds power and potential for planetary healing. Together we are exploring and revolutionizing how we embody our magic; through events, educational content, and community we aim to heal and honor the collective's relationship to the witch.

Join us in deepening our understanding of who we are as magical beings, and as a powerful collective force. Find us at *modernwitches.org*.

To Our Readers

Weiser Books, an imprint of Red Wheel/Weiser, publishes books across the entire spectrum of occult, esoteric, speculative, and New Age subjects. Our mission is to publish quality books that will make a difference in people's lives without advocating any one particular path or field of study. We value the integrity, originality, and depth of knowledge of our authors.

Our readers are our most important resource, and we appreciate your input, suggestions, and ideas about what you would like to see published.

Visit our website at *www.redwheelweiser.com*, where you can learn about our upcoming books and free downloads, and also find links to sign up for our newsletter and exclusive offers.

You can also contact us at *info@rwwbooks.com* or at

Red Wheel/Weiser, LLC
65 Parker Street, Suite 7
Newburyport, MA 01950